CREATIVE HISTORY

CREATIVE HISTORY

Second Edition

WALTER T. K. NUGENT

Indiana University

J. B. LIPPINCOTT COMPANY

Philadelphia
New York   Toronto

ISBN 0–397–47286–2

Printed in the United States of America
Cover design by Robert Perry

2 4 6 8 9 7 5 3 1

Library of Congress Cataloging in Publication Data

Nugent, Walter T   K
    Creative history.

    Includes bibliographies.
    1. History—Study and teaching.   I. Title.

D16.2.N8   1973   907'.2   73–453
ISBN 0–397–47286–2

CONTENTS

PREFACE TO THE SECOND EDITION

IN THE ROUGHLY six years since this book first appeared, it has enjoyed a considerably wider audience than I really expected it would. I never intended it as a contribution to historical theory, still less to the critical philosophy of history; treatises in these fields already existed. But I did sense a need for a pedagogical tool which would present the main problems (and current answers) involved in the practice and profession of history as plainly as possible to students beginning to encounter history at the university level. To judge from the list of those who have used this book, that need did exist. I want to thank those users (and especially those who sent me their comments and criticisms for use in preparing this second edition), not just for the ego-trip involved in seeing my hunch borne out, but more importantly for sharing my concern that history as a way of approaching reality should be explained more adequately to students.

Some of my views have changed since the first edition appeared, most noticeably, probably, in the form of increased skepticism towards objective relativism and a growing appreciation for what might be called objectivity or replicability. This shift began with reflections on the implications of some of my own research in late nineteenth-century American history, as well as research by other historians, and it was fortified in the area of theory by reading Arthur Danto's *Analytic Philosophy of History*. I think this shift is not unique with me, but, like most of the rest of the book, represents a consensus of much of the historical profession on these questions. This change will be evident, as will the updating of bibliographies and a number of points of historical method.

But I have had no intention of making this edition a completely different book from the first edition. In survey courses in western civilization, world history, and United States history, instructors found often that discussion time was short. The "background" sections in each chapter, which they therefore found useful, have been expanded. Other instructors who used the book in courses on historical methods or theory did find the "feedback" and "homework" sections useful, and thus I have retained these. For those who found what used to be the fourth chapter, on techniques of studying, somewhat interruptive of the flow of material on history itself, I have transformed that chapter into Appendix II, and those whom it helps may find it there. In sum, I have made a number of changes in response to suggestions from students and teachers. It remains true that those who seek an original contribution to the philosophy of history will not find it here, for the book was and is not intended to be that; for such a thing see Gardiner or Danto or many other writers referred to in Appendix I or elsewhere. The book is still the glorified lab manual it was meant to be, and for which purpose people have found it useful. I hope this second edition will increase its utility.

I must thank my friends Philip M. Rice, of the Claremont Graduate School, Robert H. Ferrell, of Indiana University, and Alex Fraser, formerly of the J. B. Lippincott Company, for their inspiration and suggestions; of course the use or misuse of them is entirely my responsibility. I would also like to thank the many students it has been my good fortune to teach and who have helped me understand history better by allowing me to help them understand it.

WALTER T. K. NUGENT

Bloomington, Indiana
December, 1972

TO THE INSTRUCTOR

THIS BOOK IS intended as a possible remedy for a deficiency in college-level survey courses in history sensed by many instructors in recent years. The deficiency is the failure of the survey courses to give the student much understanding of history as a discipline. Anyone who has undertaken historical research or who has prepared a set of course lectures in history knows that these things involve a creative process which takes some skill and which means making dozens or hundreds of intellectual decisions about content, style, and even fundamental philosophy. But the beginning undergraduate, presented with lectures, or a textbook, or even a textbook-cum-paperbacks, does not realize this. History is something fixed on a printed page; how it arrived there he seldom asks, and when he does ask, he can find no answer. In his beginning chemistry or zoology course he is treated to something very different. In addition to lectures which convey to him a certain body of knowledge, he finds himself in a laboratory where he must himself become involved, even if at an elementary level, with the processes by which this knowledge is arrived at. If it is important for him to know how science is *done,* shouldn't it also be worth knowing how history is *done?*

Another reason for learning about the creative aspects of history stems from growing enrollments. In every entering freshman class there are students who will go on to take an undergraduate major in history and, perhaps, even a handful who will ultimately choose historical research as a career. The earlier these people are introduced to what might be called the operative side of the discipline, the earlier will they have a realistic understanding of its nature and possibilities; the earlier, too, will they begin serious training. Perhaps the ideal way to begin such training, and also, perhaps, the ideal way to show undergraduates that history is a creative discipline, is to install in the curriculum a course devoted fully to the subject, perhaps entitled "an introduction to history." But curricula are crowded; every credit hour must produce its maximum yield. Other things, including the basic content courses, must be taught. Yet nothing surpasses creative, active history itself for attracting, retaining, and educating capable history students and future historians. To solve this problem in curricular economics, I am suggesting the incorporation of such "introduction to history" material in basic undergraduate courses.

A third reason for examining and engaging in creative history lies in the place of history among the liberal arts. History is not only a body of knowledge, but also a whole way of thinking. It is generally accepted, but much less often recognized, as such. People think historically, but for lack of training don't do it well. Regardless of how perfect a beginning history course may be in dealing intelligently with the major areas and problems of the past about which a college graduate should know, other situations are bound to arise in which the historical habit of thought will be of great use to him. If he has some clue about how to think historically about these situations, he is apt to be much better off, and so will we all. He will certainly be a better man for having read Tacitus or for having come to some terms with the French Revolution, but he will also become a better man for having learned the technique of reconstructing a complex situation or process from available and scattered evidence.

Obviously, then, this book is no substitute for a text or for class lectures. It is a supplement to them, aimed at spiking the sense of historical fixity or "givenness" that texts and lectures so often seem to convey. This said, how can it be used?

Since the ideal place for an "introduction to history" is, apparently, very early in a student's college career, this book is aimed in the first place at freshman and sophomore surveys. In institutions where the two-lecture-one-recitation-per-week system is in operation, this book can be used in the recitation sections. In smaller classes involving three lecture sessions per week, it can be used once a week, substituting for a lecture and as the basis for a full-hour or part-hour discussion. In either case it will cut into the time ordinarily spent on "content," but since it is impossible in a survey to "cover everything" anyway, and since the "how and why" of history is important too, this may be worth doing.

The sixteen sections of the book match roughly the number of weeks available for instruction in a semester. Since these sections are not strictly progressive, however, the book may be used as often or as little during a semester, quarter, or school year as the instructor sees fit. Most of the sections follow a fourfold pattern: first, a summary of what I take to be the prevailing attitude of American historians to the subject at hand, slightly embellished and, I hope, not too crotchety; second, discussion outlines which flow from the background essay and suggested reading; third, a few annotated bibliographical references; and fourth, exercises for the student to perform and which, I hope, will bring him to grips with problems historians face.

This book may also prove useful in undergraduate courses in historiography or historical method. A few high school instructors may find it suited to their needs. Some of the exercises aimed at teaching historical thinking may be of value to college advanced placement administrators as tests of aptitude for historical study; I think particularly of the exercises in sections 5, 6, 10, and 11. All of the sections will, perhaps, help students to think more historically and to see for themselves how historians operate.

TO THE STUDENT

IF YOU ARE like most people, you have some mistaken ideas about history as it is written and as it is studied as an academic subject. Most people think history is pretty well settled, and its general outlines and important aspects cut-and-dried. Most people think that historical research is a matter of filling in gaps in detail in a story already well known, and that the filling-in process simply involves gathering a number of new facts which are then subjected to a process called "interpretation." Following assumptions like these, many people become serenely overconfident about the timeless fixity of the facts and interpretations they happen to have run across. They are forever saying "history proves . . . ," or "we know from history . . . ," and the like.

If you think things like these, this book may surprise you and teach you something new. If you are one of the few, however, who has sometimes wondered whether the dichotomy between "fact" and "interpretation" is really very clear-cut, or who is aware that history is as much a matter of problems and questions as it is of events, or who has noticed that interpretations even of cataclysms such as the French Revolution or the American Civil War change and differ, then you will perhaps enjoy this book and find that you were on the right track after all. The purpose of this book is to show how history, written history, is created; how historians go about creating it; and what the chief problems are that historians encounter while functioning as historians.

Why bother? For one thing, such misconceptions about the study of history as those just mentioned should be corrected—misconceptions which up to now have not really been your fault since they are widely accepted as the truth, but which will be your fault if you refuse to think your way through them. For another thing, you will discover that a subject that many people consider boring (and with good reason, considering how history is often taught) is actually a creative enterprise involving, at this moment more than ever, as much soul-searching change and growth as any physical or social science. Finally, learning about history, as distinct from learning history, will make you think.

Let's assume that you are taking a beginning history course in college or university for some other reason than that you were forced to. Perhaps you found a history course the least objectionable way to fulfill some graduation requirement; such cynicism isn't unknown. But it really is true that there has been a steady increase in undergraduate history majors, history graduate students, career historians, and enrollments in history courses. In many places around the country, formal education in history is growing even faster than the colleges and universities that contain it.

What expectations are behind the rise in interest? Are the expectations being fulfilled? One expectation people have about history courses is that such courses will satisfy their sheer idle curiosity about the past. "I've always been intrigued with history," a professor often hears. He hears it with a touch of diffidence, because he knows that the kind of history with which the student has been intrigued has consisted mostly of good stories or patriotic symbols whose effect has not been to give the mind something to wrestle with, but to give the spirit something with which to feel comfortable. This is all right as far as it goes. But it doesn't go as far as college. There still are, to be sure, college history courses that give students a smattering of the antiquarian lore of their own culture, or some light but durable pieces of intellectual baggage to carry through life, and which "cover the important facts" about a large segment of the past, while avoiding the "gaps" with which a student might end up if he studied the subject on his own. These courses give a survey coverage. Yet when the process is over, the benefits seem frequently to be less than everyone hoped for at the start.

Why? Basically, because precollege history usually, and college history sometimes, do not present history as a creative activity. Push that one step further: why don't they? Because to admit that history is creative requires a person to ignore common sense, and most people cannot or will not do that. Common sense says that the past, since it already happened and cannot be recovered, is fixed. It's against common sense to say that the past changes. But it is also common sense to think that the sun goes around the earth once a day, from east to west, and it is against common sense to accept the fact that the earth goes around the sun. But, commonsensical or not, the latter happens to be true, and it also happens to be true that the past changes. Take it on faith for the moment. Perhaps, later in this book, you'll see how and why it is true.

The idea behind this book, then, is to correct the general but mistaken notion, which you may share at the moment, that history is safe, static, and dull. You may have the impression that history is something which was rather definitely organized and recorded before you ever got to see it, and that it is therefore something you are likely neither to add to nor to change creatively. Is history as concrete and eternal as the periodic table of the chemical elements or French irregular verbs? You may think so, but it is not. The key to the historical past is *change*. Everything that has happened went through a process of change, and recorded history itself is no exception. For this reason, history is creative. It is a process of making sense out of the evidences of the past, just as much as it is a body of knowledge already learned about the past.

The essays, discussion topics, and exercises which follow will help you find this out. Today it is more true than ever that people take the past into account when they try to make sense out of the world around them; most people find it natural to "think historically." But most people do it rather crudely. Surely "thinking historically" is worth learning systematically and with sophistication when you have the chance. This book gives you that chance. It should be a means of helping you find out how history *is* created, rather than what history *has been* created; how historians operate, rather than how they have operated in the books and lectures they have already produced.

ONE

WHAT DO WE MEAN
BY "HISTORY"?

1: BACKGROUND

WE USE THE WORD *history* very frequently, but we mean several things, all of which have in common something to do with the past. The first thing to get straight is the multiplicity of the senses in which we want to use the word *history,* and the second thing is to get some notion of what we mean by "the past."

Here are some variant uses of *history*. A car has a *history* of electrical trouble; a student has a *history* of missing examinations. The term means a series of apparently similar events, which happened in the past and which may or may not have had any relation to each other except for having happened to the same car or student. *History* here means only a collection of events strung out over a time span.

Another use of the term is much grander, but essentially not much different: we speak of the history of the universe, or earth history, or the history of the horse from *eohippus* to *equus*. Such "histories" almost always imply some kind of progression from something simple to something complex and, therefore, involve the notion of development, whereas electrical trouble in a car or a student's missing examinations may very well not.

But a car's history of trouble over a few weeks and the horse's history of development over fifty million years have one thing in common, which is crucial from our point of view: the car and the horse were *not conscious* of their own history. What happened to them was nothing more than that—happenings—because the car or horse, lacking minds, could not find meaning, sequence, or pattern in those events.

To convert "happenings" into "history," in a stricter and more meaningful sense of the term, takes a conscious and reflecting mind. Only man possesses such a thing, and, to tell the truth, he has applied his conscious and reflecting mind to his own past happenings only very sporadically until the last two hundred years or so, and he has done so far from uniformly even during that time. When we use the term *history* in educated or academic circles, we usually refrain from applying it to what has happened to cars or horses and restrict it to what has happened to people. But this is really a matter of usage which logic can defend only imperfectly. To talk of Roman history, or modern history, or Latin-American history, or economic history, is to use the term *history* in a more acceptable sense (at least to historians) than to use it with reference to cars or horses, for the simple reason that we are now talking about the past that happened to people. The academic usage of the word *history* reserves it for man's past, not the universal, inanimate, or nonhuman past. But even past things that happened to human beings do not necessarily involve consciousness; many people, in fact the majority of mankind, do not reflect and have not reflected on their own past, either to remember or record what has happened to them or to convert what has happened to them into *history* in the highest sense of the word.

To illustrate: what about our student who has a *history* of missing examinations? To use *history* in that sense is simply a verbal shorthand for saying that a string of such episodes happened to a particular person in the past. The student may very well not be conscious of these episodes forming a *history* in the second sense, that is, of a series of *related* episodes. In fact he may see these episodes as regrettable and unintended exceptions to his general rule of attending examinations. Granted that these episodes unarguably happened to a human person; but unless there is consciousness or self-consciousness involved, an application of mind which transforms these unrelated events into some pattern or other, *history* in the highest sense has not yet been called into existence.

Immediately it becomes obvious that the person who is thinking consciously about the events—namely, the historian —is important here. If the student is the historian, the significant episodes are the examinations he has attended, and those he missed were exceptions. His professor and the dean of students may look at it differently, since for them a single missed examination is too many and may indicate a syndrome of irresponsibility on the part of the student. On the face of it, this is just a difference in point of view. But student, professor, and dean are working within the same institutional framework and toward the same educational ends, and it is the latter two who are apt to prevail. The student needs to learn more about history for the sake of his self-preservation.

History, then, can mean any events or episodes that happened in the past, no matter to whom they happened and no matter whether the episodes were in any way related. More often, the term is restricted to things that happened to people. Most appropriately, however, *history* means past happenings to people, which have been reflected upon and in some way understood by a conscious mind.

Now for that other term, *the past*. The question of "what is it" sounds easy: it is everything except the present moment and that which is yet to come; it is everything that has happened prior to "right now." But this definition does not satisfy a historian, because it really only rewords the term *past*. It is like telling you that Patagonia exists and is not non-Patagonia, but it doesn't tell you where it is, how you get there, or how you can tell when you've arrived. So we have to ask, where is this past, and what does it look like? You stand there, trying to look like a historian, and you have to ask yourself, is the past under your feet, at the end of a walk to your nearest library, or inside your reflecting mind?

It is in all three places and others besides. We are certain that lots of people lived before us and that they were involved in many events. There is adequate proof for this, and much of it is obvious: old buildings, old books, and old paintings; ruins, arrowheads, and cemeteries; people's recollections; the necessity of having had parents, grandparents, great-grandparents ad infinitum. There are, then, records of the past. People have left things to remember them by. In fact these remains of the past make up one of the less widely used definitions of *history,* sometimes called *history-as-record.* These records of the past may be written (a book, an old letter or document, an epitaph on a tombstone) or oral (folk tales, songs, somebody saying "I remember when . . .") or physical (the Capitol building, a spinning wheel, the Roman Forum). Without these records, which the historian calls *sources,* the past is irrecoverable. Without a record of something having happened, we cannot know that it ever did happen. If we don't know that something happened, we can hardly reflect on it and relate it to other happenings. Hence the dictum: *no record, no history.*

On the other hand, sources may sometimes be indirect. One of the skills that historians must develop is that of "milking the sources" to get every last drop of information they may yield. For example: we know that clerical celibacy, an unmarried priesthood, was not the rule in the earliest years of the Christian Church despite its prevalence today in the Latin branch of Roman Catholicism. We know this because, along with other evidence, we know that St. Peter was married. Evidence? We have no direct evidence of St. Peter's wife, but three independent sources (the evangelists SS. Matthew, Mark, and Luke) mention St. Peter's mother-in-law. The only way to acquire a mother-in-law is by being married; hence Peter was married. This is one example of interpolation or "milking of sources."

But for much of the past, in fact most of it, we have no sources at all. For a good part of what is left, even the existing sources are out of our reach. Some of them are not yet discovered; others have been discovered but for various reasons are not accessible. The sources by which we can know the past, "history-as-record," tell us of only a small part of the whole human past that has happened, "history-as-actuality."

Add to this the requirement that reflecting minds must go to work on these records before history in the highest sense results, and you have further difficulties and a new element of uncertainty. For example, of the several billion events that must have occurred in France in the first year of the Revolution, 1789, or in the United States in the last year of the Civil War, 1865, we have record of perhaps no more than a couple of hundred thousand for each year. Even so, two hundred thousand bits of evidence are quite a few, and the mathematical chances that two reflecting minds will come up with the same assessment and arrangement of them are infinitesimal.

We will deal later with these questions, and with such related and famous questions as whether history is "objective" or whether history is a science or an art (or something else).

For the moment, however, we should remember particularly that the word *history* has a number of meanings, and so does the word *past*. First, there is the past that did happen—history in the sense of "what people have done." Second, there is the past that we can know about—history in the sense of "what people have left us to remember them by." Finally, there is the past that we have tried to make sense out of—history defined as "what people think they have done." *No record, no history,* true enough; *no thought, no history,* either.

Historians, then, are concerned with what people have done in the past. Moreover (and this is the special, unique province of historical thinking), they are concerned with change over time—how people and the institutions of all kinds that people create become transformed with the passage of time. Historians involve themselves in describing these changes, and by describing and analyzing them, they explain why the changes took place.

2: FEEDBACK

THE FOLLOWING ARE questions and problems that you should now be able to discuss. When you discuss them, use historical examples, drawn from what you are now studying in class and from your other knowledge, as often as you can.

  a. Are the terms *history* and *past* identical, opposite, unrelated, related? If they are related, how so? And does the relationship differ in the cases of the past and the history of the ancient Near East, Puritan New England, the *Ancien Régime* in France, or Reconstruction after the American Civil War?

  b. Regarding "written history," or history in the sense of what results from a historian's labors, which of the following statements best describes of what it *should* consist? In your experience, which of these statements best describes of what history *does* consist?

1. A record of all known facts about the human past or a selected chunk of it (note: *fact* and other basic terms will be discussed later).
2. A record of "important" or "significant" facts about the human past.
3. An "interpretation" of the important facts about the human past.
4. An interpretation and a recital of facts about the past at the same time (which raises the question, is it possible to recite the facts without choosing among them or interpreting them in some way?)

c. Where, primarily, does history come from? Records? The past? Historians? Libraries?

d. Here are two statements about the nature of written history. R. G. Collingwood (1889–1943), perhaps the outstanding English philosopher of history in this century and a historian as well, believed that history is present thought about the past. Leopold von Ranke (1795–1886), frequently referred to as the founder of modern historical method, said in a much-quoted phrase that history ought to be written *wie es eigentlich gewesen ist*—as it actually happened. Do you find any essential difference between the views of Collingwood and Ranke? Which makes more sense to you, or do they seem equally valid? Use examples.

3: DIGGING

AS YOU MIGHT guess, this is not the first book to discuss the nature of history. Here are some others:

Beard, Charles A. "Grounds for a Reconsideration of Historiography," in Social Science Research Council, Bulletin 54, *Theory and Practice in Historical Study* (A Report of the Committee on Historiography; New York: Social Science Research Council, 1946), pp. 1–14. Beard (1874–1948) was probably one of the three finest historians America has produced in the twentieth century. This essay is sometimes polysyllabic but never dull, and the author, as usual, presents his views forcefully.

Berkhofer, Robert. *The Behavioral Approach to Historical Analysis.* New York: Free Press, 1969. Tough going, especially at first, but ultimately an engaging and vigorous presentation of how historians should function in the light of behavioral theory and practice as developed recently in the social sciences.

Carr, Edward Hallett. *What Is History?* New York: Alfred A. Knopf, 1962. This small and readable book consists of six lectures by a leading British historian presented at Cambridge University in 1961. Carr's general outlook is somewhat akin to that of Collingwood.

Collingwood, Robin George. *The Idea of History.* New York: Oxford University Press, 1956. See especially Part V. This is, frankly, tough reading, but as Collingwood's major statement on the nature of history, it is important in itself and for its very wide influence on present-day historians.

Nevins, Allan. *The Gateway to History.* New York: D. Appleton-Century Company, 1938. Especially Chapter 2. This engaging discussion is by the former Columbia University historian.

Smith, Page. *The Historian and History.* New York: Alfred A. Knopf, 1964. With sharp mind and sharp pen, this leading California historian attacks past misconceptions and offers what he thinks are more solid ideas in their place. See Chapters 11, 13, and 14.

4: HOMEWORK

   a. On the basis of these discussions and what reading
   you may have done, write your own definition of *history* in ten words or less.

   b. Use the word *history* differently in five different sentences.

   c. Explain briefly how any one of the authors listed
   above uses *history* in a way different from the ways
   explained earlier in this section.

TWO

WHY STUDY HISTORY?

1: BACKGROUND

THERE ARE MANY reasons for studying history; some of them
are more practical than others. As often happens, some of the
reasons that seem least practical and most abstract and ideal-
istic turn out to be the most practical in the long run. A little
precision in language brings this out. The question "why study
history?" can be interpreted in two different ways. One is in
the sense of "how can it help me make a living?" The second
is in the sense of "how can it help me become a better person?"
Since making a living is only one part of life, but living with
oneself as a person is, for better or worse, full-time, the second
question is the more practical, since it affects one much more
profoundly and much more often. More of this later, however.
How, in fact, can the study of history help you make a living?

History is a very broad subject. Since it includes everything
that has happened, it is the broadest subject there is, except
perhaps philosophy. History deals with people, both humanis-
tically because of its attention to the individual person and the

unique event and scientifically because it also deals with people in groups and as the focus of long-term trends. History is also deeply involved with language and communication, not only because it concerns itself with the ways in which people have related to one another, but also because history as a subject or discipline can be set forth only through the medium of language. Consequently, because of its breadth, its concern with people and their institutions, and its essential connection with language, the study of history prepares a person for a considerable number of occupations and professions to which these qualities are central.

What, then, can you do with history? The obvious thing, once you have learned a little of it, is to pass it on. With a major or a concentration in history in college you can go out and teach history to other people, as a high school teacher. Or, if you are particularly good at it and are willing to spend several more years picking up the M.A. and Ph.D. degrees which would qualify you as a trained professional historian, you can teach at the college or university level and do historical research and writing yourself.

What is less often realized, however, is that a concentration on history in college is an excellent, generally recognized, and often ideal way to prepare yourself for many other vocations. There are a host of positions in government, especially the federal government, for which the breadth of history and the familiarity with American institutions that it can provide make an excellent preparation. The largest part of governmental intelligence work consists of research for which the techniques and subject matter of history prepare a person directly. For the few who are able enough to qualify, the diplomatic profession—called in America the Foreign Service of the United States—is a fascinating career which demands preparation in history at least equally with political science and economics.

Nor do government careers offer the only opportunities for

those trained in history. Law schools look upon a major in history as one of the best means by which a future attorney can ready himself for his professional training in law school. Undergraduate preparation in history is also one of the most effective routes to library school and a career as a professional librarian, and it also has been the field of concentration for most professional archivists who work in state, private, federal, or university archives. The National Park Service employs people with various levels of preparation in history in its task of locating and preserving the country's historic sites and monuments.

History and politics have traditionally been closely connected. Although the majority of politicians have been lawyers first, others (such as Presidents Theodore Roosevelt and John F. Kennedy, who wrote historical works) have entered politics with an academic background consisting of an undergraduate major in history. The business world, while it prefers accounting or engineering students for many of its jobs, looks for liberal arts (including history) majors for others, such as personnel and public relations positions. The advertising industry, in fact, employs many former history majors because of their combination of writing competence, familiarity with American culture, and frequent acquaintance with the skills of social research.

Newspaper and periodical journalism employs at every level thousands of people who studied history in college. Some history majors with the proper flair have made attractive careers for themselves in book publishing, particularly as editors or as publishers' agents. The vocational possibilities are really very extensive, and as this sketch indicates, there are plenty of answers to the question, "what can I do with a history major except teach?"

History, then, can help you make a living in a multitude of ways. But what about the other question asked at the start

—the more practical one—how can it help you become a better person?

The main answer to this question can be summed up in two quotations, one from the English poet Alexander Pope (1688–1744), the other from the Greek playwright Menander (342–292 B.C.). Pope, echoing a phrase that goes back at least to Plato, said, "Know then thyself, presume not God to scan; the proper study of mankind is man" (*Essay on Man,* Epistle II). From the Greeks to the present day, intelligent people have realized that if they were to do anything, build anything, or be anything that was admirable or worthwhile, they first would need to understand themselves. Without a knowledge of one's strengths and weaknesses, one's peculiarities and potential, one would never know what he could do; without a knowledge of where one came from, one would never know where he was going. But, someone objects, wouldn't the study of psychology, or perhaps having oneself psychoanalyzed, accomplish this? Menander had the answer to this. In his *Thrasyleon* the dramatist asserted, "In many ways the saying 'Know thyself' is not well said. It were more practical to say 'Know other people.'" Nowhere do you study more people in more varied circumstances than in history. Everyone is a product of his society; every society is a product of its past. To know the past and that of other people is to know yourself.

A related virtue of historical study is that it releases you from the prison of your own time. It permits you to see that life can be, and indeed was, different from what it is for us at present, and shows you a society (perhaps your own) at a different point in time, with different problems, different social structures, and different alternatives for meeting what was then the future. Of course this virtue can be short-circuited: it is always possible to refuse to look at the past except through present-sighted eyes and with present-minded expectations. But this is as silly and self-defeating as refusing to look at and evaluate another culture, except by American standards. One must look at the past, as at other cultures in the present, on its own terms, and seek to comprehend it as it existed then, without the distorting overlay of intervening events and changes.

Self-study by historical study must obviously be concerned with one's own society, which for Americans is the history of the United States and of the Western world. But it is profoundly important to study other histories too. There is too much parochialism, self-righteousness, and blind nationalism in the world, and, as the world has twice found out in the twentieth century, these attitudes can provide the climate for the horrible devastation of world war. Learning that your own national way of doing things is not the only way (and certainly not the norm for other people) and learning that the behavior of other people in other times and places is not particularly bad or unworkable because it is old or foreign is an essential revelation for any person who pretends to be educated.

History is important for other reasons too. For one thing, it is the collective experience of mankind, and as such it teaches us lessons that may help us avoid in the future some of the mistakes we have made in the past. For another thing, history shares with the other liberal arts, such as literature, philosophy, or mathematics, the virtue of being able to train us to think. This does not mean necessarily training to think about particular things, but rather training in the process of thinking, in general. A trained mind, one that is flexible and perceptive with respect to whatever new problem confronts it, is the most practical tool imaginable. History, as a mind-training discipline, has a practicality that is supreme. Another reason for studying it is that no other subject pulls together all of human experience so broadly, and no other subject relates the many parts of this experience to each other.

The following discussion subjects may help to explore some of these points more fully.

2: FEEDBACK

a. History, it was just said, provides a synthesis of knowledge and experience.

   1. If history attempts to be a synthesis of all knowledge, then why study other subjects? Wouldn't history obviate them?

   2. Name another field of study which also attempts to synthesize knowledge. How does history compare to it in approach? Which is more comprehensive?

   3. If history attempts to synthesize all knowledge, why do many history courses emphasize past politics so heavily?

b. Suppose you are a history major in your senior year in college. Considering the kinds of jobs (mentioned earlier in this chapter) that would be open to you after graduation, how would you evaluate their advantages and disadvantages; how would you go about getting the position you prefer; and how would you go about presenting your history background as an asset in a way that would impress or convince a prospective employer?

c. Since history deals with the whole of the human past, it deals with almost all of human reality. Does this also function for matters close to home? Name some events, topics, or problems in present-day society or in your own life (examples: race relations, foreign policy, the draft, the way your education is being paid for). In what sense can any of them be said to have had a history or to have been shaped by history? Have any of them *not* had some roots in the past?

d. Let us explore the term *liberal arts* and the relation history may have to it.

1. Name some fields of study which are useful for training a person to *do* some particular thing, and, then, name some fields useful for helping a person be a certain kind of person. We can call the first type training and the second type education.

2. Is there a distinction, then, between training and education? Is education practical?

3. Is history a subject that trains, or is it one that educates, or is it both? Can history be of practical use? It might have been practical for the student in Section One who missed his examination.

e. Why do you think history is required, or at least strongly suggested, for successful completion of primary, secondary, and college curricula in this and other countries? Can you suggest some practical reason, or do you attribute this practice to the sheer inertia of tradition?

f. The relation or application of the past to the present is a curious one, but it is often taken for granted. Everyone has heard the phrase, "history repeats itself."

1. Do you think the phrase is always, usually, seldom, or never true?

2. Think of any single event in history, broad or narrow (for example, World War II, Luther's revolt, Hitler's Jewish policy, Kennedy's assassination). Is it exactly like any other event you can think of? Is it completely unlike any other event? To what degree are one and another event similar or different, as to their causes, their relations to contemporaneous events, their effects, or in other ways?

3. How, if at all, can history have a predictive purpose? Can it teach us or promise us anything about the future?

3: DIGGING

THE FOLLOWING ARE some other discussions of the uses of history.

American Historical Association. *History as a Career to Undergraduates Choosing a Profession*. Washington, n.d. This is not a guide to the alternatives open to undergraduate history majors, but it is rather a good discussion of the nature and attractions of a career as a professional research historian.

Gustavson, Carl G. *A Preface to History*. New York: McGraw-Hill Book Company, 1955. In Chapters 1, 2, and 13, Gustavson shows why history is important (in fact, unavoidable) and what historians do.

Hexter, J. H. *Doing History*. Bloomington: Indiana University Press, 1971. A delightfully written discussion of contemporary historical practice.

Muller, Herbert J. *The Uses of the Past: Profiles of Former Societies*. New York: Oxford University Press, 1952. Muller, especially in the first two chapters and the last, describes elegantly what history can teach us and how this can help us.

Nevins, Allan. *The Gateway to History*. New York: D. Appleton-Century Company, 1938. With delight and conviction, the master narrative historian explains how human history helps humans.

4: HOMEWORK

a. Choose two of the courses that you are now taking other than history. List on a sheet of paper as many ways as you can in which these courses include historical material and in which a further knowledge of history would help a person to understand them.

b. List as many ways as you can in which history is involved in the activities of the following people and how further historical knowledge might assist them: the driver of a car, a voter, the parent of an eighteen-year-old, the parent of an eighteen-month-old, a businessman.

THREE

THE LIBRARY,
THE HISTORIAN'S HARDWARE

1: BACKGROUND

HISTORIANS DO NOT get all their material from libraries, but they could no more function without libraries than chemists could function without Bunsen burners, zoologists without microscopes, or nuclear physicists without nuclear accelerators. Books, periodicals, manuscripts, and statistical data are the tools of the historian's trade, and if a historian does not have an adequate library in which to work, he finds it difficult if not impossible to function. If you would know about history and historians, you must know about libraries.

College courses in scientific subjects, such as chemistry or zoology, notoriously involve many hours of laboratory work for which a student, to his dismay, is not credited with as many hours of work as he is for lecture courses. But these courses are often thought of as among the more difficult ones, and the students who major in them are often thought of as having been trained more rigorously than students who study, for the most part, the humanities or the social sciences. A large part of the reason for this is that libraries are to the historian what laboratories are to the scientist. Professional historians spend many hours in them. But because it is possible to read some books, or to sleep over them, outside a library, while it is not usually convenient to dissect a cat, run rats, or conduct a fractional distillation outside a laboratory, history students often fail to realize how necessary libraries are. As a history student, you should spend as many hours in the library as you spend in a laboratory for your science courses—possibly many more—even though you probably won't earn credits as you would in a lab.

Most people are unaware that there are great differences among libraries—differences not only of size but of function and content. The tax-supported public libraries that are such a familiar institution in American cities and towns developed only within the last hundred years and could scarcely have developed much earlier; a public school system that brought literacy to a significant number of Americans had become widespread only a few years earlier. Public libraries would be rather pointless among a population unable or unwilling to read the books in them, which is one reason why such libraries are found in only a few countries in our mostly illiterate world. Most public libraries are circulating libraries (people can borrow books from them and take them out), and since they exist to serve a general clientele, their collections as a rule are more broad than deep. This rule does not hold for a very few public libraries, which function not as ordinary municipal circulating libraries at all but as vast storehouses catering to a multiplicity of specialized research needs.

The most spectacular example of such a relatively rare giant is the New York Public Library, which houses a collection of several million volumes that received its start toward greatness from the benefactions of such wealthy New

York families as the Astors and the Tildens in the late nineteenth century. Another public library—public in the sense that it is supported by tax funds—is the Library of Congress on Capitol Hill in Washington. This splendid institution, the world's largest library with over 64 million "pieces" (not only books, but maps, manuscripts, photographs, antique musical instruments, pamphlets, and other items), got its first boost in the early nineteenth century, when former President Jefferson found it necessary in his old age to sell his private library to the government in order to meet some of his debts. The Library of Congress has been growing ever since, and although it is technically in existence to assist congressmen in planning legislation, it is open to the public. Other governments have supported such research libraries for similar purposes; those most familiar to Americans are the splendid collections of the British Museum in London and the Bibliothèque Nationale in Paris.

University libraries share some of the characteristics of all of these institutions: they exist primarily to serve the research and teaching needs of the faculty and students of the university. Consequently many of them maintain very considerable research collections, but they also permit most of their holdings to circulate among the same somewhat restricted clientele. Scholarship in America is also served by a select group of research libraries which usually specialize in certain fields or periods and cater to established scholars and advanced students. These include, among others, the Massachusetts Historical Society in Boston, the Historical Society of Pennsylvania at Philadelphia, the John Crerar Library (science and technology) in Chicago, the Newberry Library (literature, history, and other humanistic subjects for the period roughly A.D. 1300–1900) in Chicago, and the Huntington Library in San Marino, near Los Angeles.

2: ARCHIVES

ANOTHER KIND OF depository which historians find indispensable is the archive. Archives resemble libraries in most ways, but while libraries chiefly contain books, archives chiefly contain manuscripts and other unique records. In the broad sense of the term, archives are very common. Every county seat in America has them in the form of the register of deeds and tax assessor's offices; state and federal agencies, churches, colleges, business firms, and even private families have their archives, although they may not dignify file cabinets or boxes of papers· by that name. Great libraries often have archival divisions, often called manuscript sections; manuscript rooms exist, for example, in the Library of Congress, the New York Public Library, the British Museum, and most large university libraries. State historical societies, which are extremely useful depositories for all sorts of public and private records relating to state and local history, almost always have archives. Central governments, however, have the outstanding ones, and the great archives in America are the National Archives in Washington. Federal archivists also superintend the libraries (really archives) of the several most recent presidents (Roosevelt at Hyde Park, Hoover at West Branch, Truman at Independence, Eisenhower at Abilene, Kennedy at Cambridge, and Johnson at Austin). The Public Record Office in London, the Archives Nationales in Paris, and national archives in Rome, Moscow, Ottawa, and other capitals serve the same function elsewhere.

3: LIBRARY SERVICES

NOT ONLY ARE most people unaware of the variety of libraries that exist, but they are usually unaware also of the variety of services and operations that libraries perform. The work of a university research library falls into two categories, often called "readers' services" and "technical services." Most people know about parts of the former, such as the card catalog, the circulation division, the reference rooms, and the stacks where the books themselves are kept. But "readers' services" also include an interlibrary loan section whose job it is to borrow from elsewhere books that the library does not have and which a reader needs, reference librarians who help a reader to find something the library does have but which the reader cannot find by himself, microfilm reading rooms, a photocopying service, book-form or card-form catalogs of other libraries, and other sections. "Technical services," like the submerged part of an iceberg, keep the visible part of the library afloat but cannot be seen unless one looks underwater. They decide what books to buy, buy them, catalog them and see that they get to the shelves, repair worn or damaged volumes, and supervise the financing and staffing of the library. A sizable university research library will today have a staff of well over a hundred people, but even a frequent reader may see no more than a dozen of these people. Without the whole staff, libraries could not operate, and without libraries and archives, historians could not operate.

4: HOMEWORK

  a. University libraries do not differ radically in the kinds of services they perform, but they do differ in physical layout.
     1. Walk around the various sections of your college library, and be prepared to state where principal divisions of the library are.
     2. What library resources are there in your home

community which would help you as a history researcher?

3. List the steps by which a book gets from its publisher or out-of-print bookseller to the shelf in your library. (You may need to go to the main library and consult a book on library practice to answer this one.)

b. In the reference room or rooms of your college library, locate ten reference works that should be useful to you as a history student. Make a list of these works, giving (i) author, (ii) title, (iii) edition number, (iv) number of volumes if more than one, (v) place of publication, publisher, and date of publication, (vi) sponsoring organization, if any, and (vii) the chief ways in which the work might be useful. (Note: Many of these works will not be shelved in the history section. Do not overlook, for example, encyclopedias, periodical indexes, atlases, statistical compilations, and biographical guides.)

Example: U.S. Department of Commerce. Bureau of the Census. *Historical Statistics of the United States, Colonial Times to 1957.* (List items iii and iv are not applicable.) Washington: Government Printing Office, 1961. "Prepared by the Bureau of the Census with the Cooperation of the Social Science Research Council." Useful for providing data for any historical study on social and economic topics, such as population, labor, business, immigration, health, education, etc.

c. The card catalog is the key to the library's resources. Find each of the following works in the card catalog of your library. List each separate item of information given on the card for each work (there may be more than a dozen pieces of information on each card):

1. Your textbook or any book catalogued under history.

2. Any volume of the *Congressional Record* or of a foreign government publication.

3. Any volume of the *American Historical Review* or of a foreign historical journal (e.g., the *Canadian Historical Review, Cahiers d'Histoire Mondiale, Archiv für Reformationsgeschichte, Voprosy istorii, Rassegna storica del Risorgimento,* etc.).

d. Certain terms are in common use in libraries. Write brief definitions of the following terms, as they are used in libraries:

stack	microfiche
serial	recall
volume and tome	carrel
call number	call slip
microfilm	Union List
microcard	interlibrary loan

e. Different libraries have different cataloguing systems. The two most commonly in use in the United States are the Library of Congress system and the Dewey decimal system. Certain libraries, such as the New York Public, have unique systems; foreign libraries use their own; and some American libraries with special strengths in certain areas have developed special variations and extensions of the Library of Congress or Dewey systems.

1. What, in general, are the differences between the Library of Congress and Dewey systems?

2. Which of these, or what other system, does your college library use? Are there any special exceptions, such as for documents?

3. Does your college library have separate card cata-

logs for subject headings and for titles and authors, or is there a single card catalog? Does your library have any special catalogs, such as for rare books, manuscripts, or special collections?

4. What classification number or letters does your college library use to identify and place books in these categories?

American history	railroads in Arkansas
medieval history	railroads in Africa
transportation	Charles the Great
Theodore Roosevelt	(Charlemagne)
Franklin Roosevelt	Charles II
Eleanor Roosevelt	Charleston, W. Va.
Roosevelt Library	Charles de Gaulle
railroads	

f. Libraries differ in size, quality, function, and kinds of collections.

1. How large is your college library? Does it have any special or unusual collections? Could you use it to do research on the French Revolution, on the Taiping Rebellion, and on American civil rights laws? If not, where could you do research on these subjects?

2. Look up and list the six largest libraries in the United States and four major libraries abroad, and give their approximate size.

3. What are the major differences between your college library and a public library?

g. Reference works such as encyclopedias and dictionaries are handy for finding quick and easy answers to factual problems. Are they authoritative? In the reference room of your library, check four or five encyclopedias and other reference works such as almanacs and see whether they agree on the size of the Principality of Monaco. (A writer in the *New York Times* recently got some interesting results when he did this.)

h. In what order does the card cataloguing system of your college library put a surname, the name of a place, the name of an association, and a title, when they all begin with the same word (e.g., Williams College, George Williams, Williamsburg, Williamstown Chamber of Commerce, William of Orange)?

i. Does your library's card catalog list a "von" or "de" name alphabetically under those words or the word following? How does it deal with "Mc" and "Mac" names?

j. Reference librarians are a long-suffering breed whose job it is to locate elusive materials and find answers to stubborn questions—stubborn to you, but not to them. Do not hesitate to consult one of these people if you still cannot find something in a library after you have made a reasonable search. Experienced scholars need their help from time to time; so will you.

FOUR

VARIETY IS THE
SPICE OF HISTORY

1: THE HISTORICAL PROFESSION AND ITS DOMAIN

THERE ARE ABOUT twenty thousand professional historians in the United States and an unknown number of nonprofessional ones, and they concern themselves with the history of every area and period in the history of the world.

Academic history in American higher education is still generally segregated into three categories—American, European, and "the rest," otherwise known as "non-Western"—which is only slightly less myopic a division than that of the secondary schools into "American" and "world" history. At both the college and secondary levels, however, the last is least, and probably should not be, if one of the chief purposes of history, the striking down of cultural or national parochialism, is to be achieved. But historians have always been among the more conservative of academics and have stressed American history, for obvious reasons, and the history of Western Europe, since that was where the profession started and was first introduced to American students in the nineteenth century.

Such preoccupation with the history of the United States and Western Europe has also dictated a division of history into the three time periods of ancient, medieval, and modern, although this trifurcation really fits only the two "Western" branches of history. We can apply these period terms to other areas, as in speaking of "medieval Russia," which ended with Peter the Great rather than 250 years earlier as medieval times did farther west, or the "middle ages" of Middle Eastern Islamic civilization, which may be going on right now, or the colonial period of Latin American history, which ended almost fifty years later than did the colonial period in the United States. This is to say nothing of East Asia or of Africa, where the historical periodizations derived from Western experience make hardly any sense at all. "Non-Western" history, however, has been coming into its own at a very rapid rate, especially during the past twenty years. It is now not uncommon to find the catalogs of even relatively small colleges listing courses in Asian, Russian, Byzantine, African, Near Eastern, Latin American, and other "exotic" histories where none except American and European history courses were to be found even a decade ago.

There are many reasons for this widening of curricular horizons. One is the growing awareness among Americans that there is more to the world (and there always has been) than just themselves and the European culture from which they sprang. But whatever the causes, the effects are laudable. Many colleges and universities, in fact, have expanded not only their history offerings but their libraries and their language programs as well, so that in some places it is as ordinary for a student to prepare himself in Russian or Chinese or Swahili, in order to study Russian or Asian or East African history, as it once was to become familiar with French and German in order to study European history. The trend will doubtless continue.

Historical study in the United States has expanded in recent years to include different kinds of problems as well as different areas of the world. Very much limited until recently to the study of past politics, historians and historical study in America now usually include social, intellectual, cultural, economic, demographic, and other material, while maintaining the traditional focus on politics. As a result, the study of history in America today is not only a background for political science, but also for sociology, anthropology, economics, literature, geography, and other subjects. History departments still put considerable stress on the more traditional kinds of history, such as political and diplomatic, and on the very traditional areas of military and constitutional, especially in American history. But, on the other hand, a great many departments have moved vigorously in recent years into economic, social, intellectual, and cultural history, and at the same time they have redefined their emphasis on fields to include the "non-Western" cultures and comparative history.

In some of the leading institutions in the country, history has come to play a key role in the development of area studies, which train students—undergraduates or graduates—in many aspects of a particular culture, so that they may become "area specialists." At one major midwestern university, for example, undergraduate or graduate students may concentrate in the history of Russia, at the same time gaining fluency in the Russian language and taking training in Slavic literature, Russian and Soviet economics, Russian and Soviet government and law, Russian music and folklore, the Soviet educational system, and the sociology of Slavic and West Asian areas. If a student wishes, he may familiarize himself with supporting work in East European or Byzantine or medieval Russian history, the history and culture of the non-Russian parts of the Soviet Union in central and eastern Asia, and even learn Uzbek, Mongol, Tibetan, or Turkish, and the scientific linguistics to go with them. Area studies programs, with history at their core, exist in American universities today to deal in a similarly comprehensive way with Latin America, Africa, the Near and Middle East, Southeast Asia, and East Asia.

All of this seems a far cry from the traditional survey courses in Western civilization and the history of the United States. But the distance is shorter than you may think. This year's student in "Western civ" or beginning American history may be next year's student of African history, together with beginning Arabic and African physical geography, and in a few more years he may be a thoroughly trained African area specialist with his home base (intellectually) in African history and his home base (physically) in a Volkswagen crossing the savannas of west-central Africa, collecting documents and artifacts in sun-drenched multilingual trading towns and starting to formulate the definitive book on a large but little-known area of mankind's existence.

Although professional history in the United States is located chiefly in colleges and universities and remains academically oriented, it does have nonacademic or semiacademic associations. In the first place, by no means all historians are professors. Although, as a rule, the history written in the United States (certainly the most theoretical history) is written by academic historians, there are a number of very able and even eminent historians who do not have academic appointments. Mrs. Barbara Tuchman, who has written on the origins and early history of World War I and on American policy in China, is such a person. Bruce Catton, the author of many highly competent and highly popular books on the American Civil War, is another. In other countries too, most familiarly perhaps in Britain and Western Europe, the nonacademic historian is a well-known figure. In America in the past twenty years, still a third kind of historian has taken his place beside the historian-professor and the historian–freelance writer, and that is the research historian who is attached to a government agency or to a private or semiprivate research institution. The Atomic Energy Commission, the Department of the Interior, and parts of the Department of Defense have engaged historians in recent years to write their histories, and although some of these people are really academicians only temporarily away from the campus, others make a life's career in governmental history. The rise of private foundations, which has happened largely since World War II, has contributed to the establishment of large-scale research projects all over the world, which often maintain connections—but in practice only tenuous ones—with universities.

All of these developments, which together constitute the expansion of the historical profession in the past twenty years, have not been without theoretical and practical problems. While some historians will take up a new venture, such as area studies, if the funds are available, and will not stop to argue the theoretical implications, these implications have nevertheless existed. A few of them are worth discussing, because they shed some light on the nature of history and the ways it may be defined.

2: FEEDBACK

  a. History and language study. We have already discussed the necessity of records for the reconstruction of the past. It is also true that books exist today in English which deal with the history and culture of most of the areas of the world.

  1. How essential is a knowledge of the languages of an area or period to the competent study of it?
  2. What languages would be necessary for the conduct of original research in the history of medie-

val Europe, of the Byzantine Empire, of Latin America, of the Soviet Union, of East Asia?

3. Are foreign languages useful or necessary for the study of United States history—particularly for American foreign relations, immigration, or the history of American city life?

4. Suppose you contemplate becoming a close student of the history and culture of a foreign area, such as Western Europe or Russia. In what ways would it be helpful to you to visit that area? Why might it be essential to visit the area? Would it be possible to gain a really sound knowledge of it without visiting it? If you did visit it, how would a knowledge of its language help?

b. *The history of other cultures.* The preceding section on the uses of history discussed the point that one of history's most important uses was self-knowledge, which means, in large part, knowledge of other people. What are the relative advantages and disadvantages of studying one's own regional or national history without comparing it to the history of other cultures? Would it illuminate the American experience with urbanism, industrialism, or imperialism, for example, to compare it with the experience of Britain, Germany, or Russia? On the other hand, is it of no value to study one's own culture without reference to others?

c. *The varieties of history: history and politics.* The noted British historian Edward A. Freeman (1823–1892) once remarked that history is past politics, and politics is present history. This view is less popular today.

1. Glance quickly over the bibliography in your textbook. Aside from reference works, what are

some of the books listed there which do not appear to be concerned primarily with "past politics"?

2. Of the chapters in your textbook which you read
most recently, what percentage, roughly, would
you say did not deal with "past politics," and
what percentage did?

3. What are some of the nonpolitical areas dealt
with by your textbook author and in the books
listed in your textbook bibliography?

d. *History and human experience.* Sociologists point
out that each of us, in our complex society, has associations with a great many groups, institutions, and persons. For example, we each have some relation to the
educational institution of which we are members; to
our country; to the marketplace for our skills; to a
church, perhaps; to our family; to our friends, and
usually there are several circles of them. As persons
we have different kinds of experiences, private and
public, flowing from our relations with each and all
of these groups. Do historians or should historians
deal with all of these various forms of human experience, or should they concentrate mostly on "past politics"? Does "past politics" have any importance for
us? How wide, in other words, should the historian
cast his net?

e. *Is the past a seamless fabric?* Presumably if people
relate in so many ways to each other and to so many
"impersonal" institutions, such as church, country,
college, or marketplace, at the present time, then such
complex relationships existed for people in the past—
depending, of course, on the complexity of the society
in which they lived. Each person in the past presum-

ably lived many different lives: his economic life; his
family life; his life as a Moose, Elk, or Odd Fellow;
his life as a citizen; his life as a Christian or Jew or
Muslim or Buddhist; and so forth. In physical fact he
was living only one life, but in social fact he was living
many.

  1. If this is so, can we justifiably isolate one aspect
     of past existence from all the rest of it and write
     or study the history of that one aspect alone?
  2. What techniques or guidelines are there which
     can help us segregate areas of human experience
     into manageable segments? What are some of
     these segments?

3: DIGGING

THERE ARE A number of books that deal with the historical
profession and give an idea of the variety of history today.
Here are a few of the best:

Daedalus, issues of Winter 1971 and Spring 1971, entitled
   "Historical Studies Today" and "The Historian and the
   World of the Twentieth Century." The quarterly journal of
   the American Academy of Arts and Sciences devoted these
   two issues entirely to essays by two dozen leading American
   and European historians who discuss aspects of the craft.
Higham, John. *Writing American History: Essays on Modern
   Scholarship.* Bloomington: Indiana University Press, 1970.
   See especially Chapter 9, "American Historiography in the
   1960s."
Higham, John, with Leonard Krieger and Felix Gilbert. *History.* Englewood Cliffs, N.J.: Prentice-Hall, 1965. Espe-

cially the first part, in which Higham provides a first-rate history of the historical profession in the United States since it began in the late nineteenth century.

Nevins, Allan. *The Gateway to History*. New York: D. Appleton-Century Company, 1938. Although this admirable book is now thirty-five years old, it conveys the variety and fascination of historical study.

(Education and World Affairs, Inc.). *The University Looks Abroad: Approaches to World Affairs at Six American Universities*. New York: Walker and Company, 1965. Though concerned with the general (not only pertaining to history) international activities of six leading American universities, this survey shows clearly the central position of history in international studies and the importance of area studies and an international approach to the study of mankind.

4: HOMEWORK

a. Go to the card catalog of your university library and examine the sections dealing with United States history and Chinese history. What classifications other than history (which is D, E, or F in the Library of Congress system, 900 and up in the Dewey decimal system) appear among the books included there? Consult the library's classification index (a reference librarian can locate it for you) to find the subjects to which these letters or numbers refer. This will give you an idea of the scope of present-day American historical writing. (Among the examples which you are likely to run across is the classification HT, urban sociology, which includes the history of cities (Library of Congress system), and 380 (Dewey system), commerce, including business history.

b. Do the same for a cross-cultural topic such as industrialism or nationalism. List a half-dozen books dealing cross-culturally with one of these problems and not specially related to the United States.

c. Does your college or university have any special resources for area studies or for the historical study of certain international areas? Get some idea of the resources that exist and be prepared to discuss them at your next class meeting.

FIVE

FACTS AND SOURCES

1: FACTS—WHAT THEN?

MOST PEOPLE BELIEVE that history really consists of a large number of solid facts, which certain more-or-less biased people have accumulated and arranged in some kind of order, usually chronological. They think that to learn history means to memorize the "important" facts and to avoid as far as possible the biases of the arrangers. First come the facts, and then, as a kind of necessary evil, the interpretation. Journalists seem to be especially prone to this line of thinking: go out and get the facts, then write them up. The more common view among historians and philosophers of history today is that, paradoxical though it may seem, the interpretation comes first, and the facts are located and deemed important—i.e., they are selected from the vast mass of available data and organized coherently—to the degree that they fit the interpretation. But this is not by any means the same as saying that interpretations are completely arbitrary and a priori, and that facts are dredged up as proof in the way a lawyer marshals evidence to support a brief for his client. Nor would it even be possible, strictly speaking, for a good historian to operate that way if he wanted to.

The reason why he could not is simply that facts are not self-evident. The good historian makes contact with the past through the medium of his sources. The sources provide evidence that certain events took place. A fact is a statement about an event, and is not itself an event; thus, in order for a fact to exist, someone functioning as a historian must discover, from a source, that an event occurred, and then make a statement about that event. That statement becomes a "fact." Since different examiners of a source might make different statements about the same event which they become aware of from a source, the same event may engender several "facts" concerning it. For example: St. Bede's *History of the English Church and People* states, concerning events of the year 635, that "King Sigbert . . . entered a monastery that he had founded, and after receiving the tonsure, devoted his energies to winning an everlasting kingdom." Bede's statement (which is already a statement about events, not the actual events; we are already at one remove from the past, which we only know about because Bede, functioning as a historian, wrote something about it) permits several other statements, all of which are facts, and true ones, assuming Bede was accurate; these facts include such statements as: Sigbert was king in 635; before 635 Sigbert founded a monastery; religious values were, on balance, more important to Sigbert than royal prerogatives; it was customary for monks, even royal ones, to receive tonsure in order to be admitted to the monastic life. A later historian may relate facts—i.e., make statements—about what Sigbert did in 635 on the basis of what Bede wrote earlier. Which statement or statements the later historian chooses to make depends on what he is writing or researching about (e.g., a list of kings for genealogical or chronological purposes, a biography of Sigbert, the place of religion or monasticism in early Anglo-Saxon England, medieval monastic practices).

Thus the problem of which comes first, the facts or the interpretation, begins to resolve itself in a common-sense way: the facts become significant and the intepretation begins to take shape at the same time. What really happens in the constructing of a conscious and coherent history of some problem or event in the past is a process describable as "feedback." Feedback, in this sense, means something different from mutual discussion and gradual understanding, which is how we have been using it in this book. Now we use the word to signify another dialogue, one between the historian and his sources, a process by which the mind selects ever more accurately the sources that have significant meaning and relation to each other and at the same time refines the questions which the mind needs to ask of the sources. Much the same process operates in the social (and even the physical) sciences: the historian begins with an explanatory model of past events. Initially the model is crude and parts of it irrelevant to what he shortly or ultimately finds the structure of the past to have been. Through interaction of data and mind, the explanatory model is revised and refined—on an empirical basis, which is to say a progressive correction by means of discovering the significance of specific pieces of data.

The historian knows enough about a past problem to raise a question about it or to find some inconsistency, error, or gap in the existing accounts of it. He poses his question and then goes to the available sources (see below) to find some answers. When he has examined some sources, he will usually find that his questions need rephrasing; they were too blunt or uninformed in their original shape. Contact with the sources has fed back information to the historian's mind which enables him to look at his problem more subtly. The process of feeding back information from the sources, the rephrasing of questions to ask of the sources, and the answers the sources provide goes on until the historian's mind is satisfied that he has asked the most intelligent questions he can and has found the best answers he can. As new facts appear, old ones take on new significance and are discovered to have relationships previously unseen. Another historian may start at a slightly different place, with a slightly different question, and may consider certain relationships or bodies of fact more important than would another historian. But the likelihood is—if the two historians apply their conscious minds to the sources diligently enough and proceed through enough sources so that the feedback process works itself through to a point of diminishing returns—that the similarity of their answers to the same original questions will be fairly close. But this is getting into another question, that of the "objectivity" of history. That question, as well as the question of the nature of sources, will be taken up shortly. First it is worth discussing the three related terms, *fact, interpretation,* and *generalization,* which often puzzle people but which are essential to historical work.

2: PUTTING THE FACTS TOGETHER

    a. Facts and their location. Here are two problems, one chosen from the context of American history and one from modern European history, which reveal some things about "facts."

       1. On Good Friday, April 14, 1865, many things happened to Abraham Lincoln. A few of them were recorded by observers or by the President himself; a very few are thought "significant" today by historians. One of them is known and thought important by every educated American.

    (a) What are some of these facts (as given in your text, or elsewhere) and especially the very important ones?

    (b) Using "historical imagination," which for the moment we can define as "rethinking yourself backward into the past situation," think of some facts, of which we have no record or at least of which you have no knowledge, which almost had to have occurred in Lincoln's life on that day, simply because he was a human being, or because he lived in Washington, or because he was president (e.g., he probably got out of bed that morning after sleeping in the White House).

    (c) Likewise using "historical imagination," think of some facts which might possibly have occurred in Lincoln's life that day (perhaps illness, a stiff neck which made it hard for him to move quickly, problems of office which made him drowsy or distracted at the theater, etc.).

    (d) Of all the facts about Lincoln's life on that day which might have happened, probably happened, or were recorded as having happened, what percentage, roughly, fall into the latter category of facts of which we have definite record? What does this suggest as to the realistic limits of historical study?

2. If you are studying the history of Western civilization, you will be able to ask the same kinds of questions with regard to Julius Caesar's activities in and near the Roman Forum on the Ides of March, 44 B.C., or with regard to a large group of people, such as Lenin, Trotsky, and the whole

population of St. Petersburg in November, 1917.
Try asking them.

b. *Interpretation and significance.* Whether one discusses Lincoln's assassination, Caesar's assassination, or the Bolshevik Revolution, one faces certain problems of historical interpretation.

1. Why did all of the people who observed Lincoln, Caesar, or Lenin on those various fateful days record relatively so few of their activities?

2. Why are we justified in calling those days fateful? Why did people at the time choose to record certain things but not others?

3. With regard to the Lincoln problem, let us assume that the events of April 14, 1865, were described by President Lincoln, by Mrs. Lincoln, by Secretary of State William H. Seward, by General Robert E. Lee, by the White House butler, by John Wilkes Booth, and by the Ford's Theater usher. Would these accounts differ? How and why? Would the recorder's point of view, sometimes called more elaborately his "frame of reference," make any difference in his selection of facts or in the way he arranged them?

c. *Generalization.* In an earlier section, we spoke of the derivation of a "history" from an apparently unconnected series of events—the discovery, by a conscious mind, that there was something that all of those events (or persons, or historical problems such as wars or revolutions) had in common. Usually the term *generalization* has a different connotation from the term *interpretation,* but perhaps you will see from the following discussion questions that they are quite similar in important respects. Again, let us take the American presidency first and then consider several international questions.

1. What most of us would agree was the most important thing to have happened to President Lincoln on April 14, 1865, also happened to Presidents William Henry Harrison, Warren G. Harding, and Franklin D. Roosevelt, on various dates in 1841, 1923, and 1945, respectively. Presumably the events in the lives of these other presidents were just as numerous and complex as those in Lincoln's. But all of them in common had one memorable thing happen on those various days. What was it? In other words, what accurate generalization can be made about events that happened to each of those four men on four days spread over 104 years and to the United States?

2. Events now regarded as significant and which were highly complex and drawn-out began to occur in France in 1789, in China in 1911, and in Russia in 1917. What did these three events have in common with each other? All have been called "revolutions," and "revolutions" also took place in China in 1949 and Cuba in 1959; these two had common elements and were both similar and different from the previous three sets of events. What might some of these similarities and differences be? (These are examples of more complex generalizations.)

3. Historians would now generally agree that there are different kinds of generalizations, depending on one's viewpoint. Some generalizations are in the form of labels, such as "tall" or "German" people; some are periodizations, such as "modern" dancing or "sixteenth-century" painting; some simply are types or classes of things, such

as "democracy," a type of government, or "socialism," an economic system. Consider the following pairs of people: Julius Caesar and Nero; Henry VIII of England and the Emperor Charles V; Herbert Hoover and Franklin D. Roosevelt; Winston Churchill and Franklin D. Roosevelt.

(a) What generalizations could be made about each of the four pairs of people?

(b) What generalizations could be made about all seven of these people? (Aside from the generalizations hidden in the question—that all of them were people and all of them can be generalized on.)

3: SOURCES

THE HISTORIAN'S RAW materials are called *sources*. The term means the pieces of information and often also the places where the information may be found that the historian searches for, compiles, analyzes, and combines with other information in order to provide his history with its grounding in past reality.

Some books about historical method distinguish what they call "primary sources" and "secondary sources," and the distinction, regardless of the terms used, is important. A "primary source" is some direct record left behind from the period or by the people who are the subject of the historian's study. It is the actual record which has survived from the past. It was primary sources to which we referred in the first section of this book—records that may be written (a ledger, an inscription, a notebook, a volume of census figures, or a printed book) or oral (a folktale or a reminiscence) or physical (a building or a painting), but in any case the records without which history is impossible. Many historians call these simply *sources* or *documents* and leave the *primary* out of it.

A *secondary source,* which many historians prefer not to call a source at all, but a *secondary material* or a *commentary,* is an indirect record, something written *about* the period or people under study, rather than *by* them. While a primary source usually dates from the time of the events being studied, a secondary source usually dates from a later time.

A couple of examples should demonstrate the difference and should also point up the important fact that the same item may be a primary source in one context and a secondary source in another. The Declaration of Independence, written by Thomas Jefferson and approved in the Continental Congress in 1776, is a primary source for anyone who writes a history of the American Revolution or of American political ideas. Carl Becker's book, *The Declaration of Independence,* originally published in 1922, is a stimulating commentary on the document, but as a commentary, it is a "secondary work" on the Revolution, on American political ideas, and on the Declaration itself. No one interested in these three historical subjects can afford to ignore Becker's book, since it is one of those rare books that are truly indispensable to the study of a subject, despite the fact that the events it discusses were one and a half centuries old when it was written. The same could be said of Charles A. Beard's very influential book, *An Economic Interpretation of the Constitution,* first published in 1913. The Constitution drawn up at Philadelphia in 1787 is a primary source for the study of late eighteenth-century American history or for the history of American and comparative government or for American law; Beard's book is a secondary work on these subjects. In quite another context, however, Beard's and Becker's books may be useful as primary sources. Both men were interesting people about whom biographies have been written; their impact on the historical profession has been great; they played influential roles in the reform movements that swept America in the early twentieth century. For these reasons, their books are primary sources for biographers of the men themselves, for historiographers, and for historians of recent American intellectual history. The same item can thus be "primary" in one context and "secondary" in another.

The usefulness of sources rests on their reliability, and their reliability varies greatly. An eyewitness account, for example, will not often tell how closely its author was personally involved with the events he describes, how much of the events under discussion he chose to mention, whether he was really a witness to the events or got his knowledge by hearsay, or whether or not he was biased. The account may mention these things, but it will need to be verified by other accounts and records. The trained historian dealing with a primary source is a paragon of skepticism, trusting nothing except, ultimately, his own judgment. There is the possibility, in many cases, that a source may have been forged, or changed inadvertently, or parts of it omitted if it is not in its original form. There is a story about a highly respected literary scholar who wrote an extended essay on the meaning of one of Shakespeare's plays. He rested the main point of his essay on the evidence of one critical passage. The passage was indeed critical, but not in the way the scholar thought. On examination of original texts the passage turned out to be a later interpolation, and the scholar's elaborate case had been resting on a misprint. Such disasters are the scholar's sauna bath: they shake you up at the time, but the effect is salutary in the long run.

The historian, then, must himself pass judgments of many kinds on the sources he uses. Not only does he have to ask whether a document is really what it purports to be—an official publication of Congress, or a thirteenth-century inscription, or a Shakespeare first folio—but he must also ask whether the person or persons who wrote it knew what they were talking about or had any personal bias or perhaps financial interest in amending the story. All this is completely aside from the equally crucial question of whether a given source is useful and relevant for what he wants to do. The historian, in addition to locating his sources, taking and compiling notes from them, and deciding whether each of them is in any way useful for what he is writing, must evaluate the sources in many different ways. After he finds a source and applies all of these tests, he may let it become one of the thousands of similarly processed pieces of source information he must have in order to write his history, for he knows that no sources mean no history; poor sources mean poor history.

4: SOURCES AND JUDGMENT

THE DISTINCTION BETWEEN primary and secondary sources, frequently a narrow one, and the problem of the credibility and reliability of sources, appear in the following questions for discussion.

   a. Which of the following are primary sources, and which are secondary? Which might be used either way —and how and by whom?

   1. An annual report of the General Motors Corporation to its stockholders.

   2. An article on China in a 1950 issue of the *Saturday Evening Post*.

   3. An article on China in a 1950 issue of *Jenmin Jih Pao* (the publication of the Chinese Communist party, Peking).

   4. Articles on China in *Pravda* in 1950 and in 1966.

5. An article on China in the *American Political Science Review*.

6. A news story in a 1900 issue of the *Times* (London).

7. "I Hear America Singing," by Walt Whitman.

8. A report on conditions in Poland by a committee of the Congress.

9. A report on western water resources, by a committee of the Congress.

10. A speech reported in the *Congressional Record*.

11. A Senate vote reported in the *Congressional Record*.

12. A letter written by a relative from the front in World War II.

13. A letter by a Japanese soldier from the front in World War II.

14. The motion picture *Gone with the Wind*.

15. *Profiles in Courage*, by John F. Kennedy.

16. The federal census of population for 1960.

17. A Gallup poll.

   b. With regard to items 6, 8, 9, and 15:

1. Rank these items as sources according to their reliability.

2. Explain briefly why you rank them as you do.

3. *Profiles in Courage* makes statements about United States Senator Edmund Ross, who lived about a century ago. List some other sources that might help you evaluate the accuracy of Kennedy's statements about him.

5: DIGGING

THERE ARE A number of works that deal with the relation of

historians to their facts and sources. Some of them are mentioned below. Becker's and Carr's discussions are for general readers; the others are by philosophers and tend to be recondite, but they are worth looking at.

Becker, Carl L. *Everyman His Own Historian.* New York: F. S. Crofts and Company, 1935. See especially the title essay, which was Becker's presidential address to the American Historical Association in 1931.

Carr, Edward H. "The Historian and His Facts," Chapter 1 in *What Is History?* New York: Alfred A. Knopf, 1961. Pages 3–35.

Gottschalk, Louis, ed. *Generalization in the Writing of History.* A Report of the Committee on Historical Analysis of the Social Science Research Council. Chicago: University of Chicago Press, 1963. The most extended treatment (among the works cited here) of the similarities and differences between generalization and interpretation.

Hook, Sidney, ed. *Philosophy and History.* New York: New York University Press, 1963. Especially the section by Ernest Nagel.

Walsh, W. H. *Philosophy of History: An Introduction.* New York: Harper and Brothers, 1960. Especially Chapters 4 and 5.

SIX

HISTORICAL INFERENCE

1: BACKGROUND

In the opening section we discussed briefly the nature of
sources and the skill, so necessary for historians, of "milking
the sources"—analyzing the primary documents to glean
from them the greatest amount of information they will yield.
Close examination of the sources is also essential to the feedback process by which the historian reformulates the questions he is asking of the past. Without a kind of historical inference which makes the sources alive to him and which makes
him sensitive to a slight nuance or turn of phrase that a less
well-trained person might ignore, a historian could never begin to rethink the past and recreate it. Just as Indians who
spent their lives on the Great Plains were amazingly able
to identify people, animals, and natural objects at great
distances when untrained visitors saw practically nothing
at all, a historian accustomed to dealing with certain kinds
of sources sees things that the casual observer does not see.
But this is not only a matter of training. It is also a knack.

The ability to see in a document shades of meaning and suggestions of ideas and events, to sense implications wider than the statements in the document itself, to use the document to "think oneself back into the past," is essential to historical craftsmanship. German philosophers of history have given this ability the name *verstehen,* and we usually call it in English *historical understanding.* We don't imagine things that aren't there, and we don't ignore the sources and "imagine" a past out of sheer flights of fancy. But we do scour the sources for the meaning implicit in them. *Verstehen,* or understanding, or imaginative rethinking of the past—whatever it is called—essentially involves an honest effort, informed by the sources as far as is possible and useful, to understand the point of view and plausible motivations of the person or people in the past whose actions we are analyzing. It has inherent difficulties; as Berkhofer pointed out, we are less likely to understand someone's motives and actions the farther away in time and place we are from him; moreover, we have only limited ways of checking whether our understanding of his actions and motives are right. We must be careful about the ways in which the past person or group acted in an intentional, rational manner; about whether his or their actions were irrationally motivated; about whether those actions turned out very differently from how the person or people intended or expected. We must be aware that people's behavior, in the present as well as in the past, does not always accord with people's intentions about how they will behave, or with their rationalizations about how and why they did behave. If an empirically verified general theory of human motivation and action existed, historical certainty might be achieved by checking interpretations of past behavior against that theory. Since such a general theory is not now available (and it is doubtful that it ever will be), historical inference and interpretation must, in the final analysis, rest upon extreme care in relating events to each other by means of entertaining a range of interpretive models, refining and rejecting them through consideration of the known sources, and settling upon one. The danger is obviously present that the interpretive model finally arrived at will be culture-bound or subjective. But in a surprising number of practical cases the danger will be minimal—or at least slight enough to permit us to understand a segment of the past in a reasonably useful way.

The following exercises may help you grasp how, at least in its earlier stages, historical inference takes place.

2: FEEDBACK

   a. This is an excerpt from the American Declaration of Independence (1776):

1 We hold these truths to be self-evident, that all men are
2 created equal, that they are endowed by their Creator with
3 certain unalienable Rights, that among these are Life, Lib-
4 erty, and the pursuit of Happiness. That to secure these
5 rights, Governments are instituted among Men, deriving
6 their just powers from the consent of the governed, That
7 whenever any form of Government becomes destructive of
8 these ends, it is the Right of the People to alter or to
9 abolish it, and to institute new Government. . . . [The
10 "present King of Great Britain" has done, among other
11 things, the following:] He has dissolved Representative
12 Houses repeatedly, for opposing with manly firmness his
13 invasions of the Rights of the people. . . . He has affected
14 to render the Military independent of and superior to the
15 Civil Power. He has combined with others to subject us to
16 a jurisdiction foreign to our constitution, and unacknow-
17 ledged by our laws; giving his Assent to their acts of pre-
18 tended legislation:. . . . For cutting off our Trade with

19 all parts of the world: For imposing taxes on us without
20 our Consent: For depriving us in many cases, of the benefits
21 of Trial by Jury. . . .

1. Do the excerpted lines give any indication of the
   following, either in tone or content? If so, state
   on which line and by which words: (a) partisan-
   ship, (b) differences in language usage from
   present usage, (c) the truth of these statements
   themselves (is any document its own proof?).
2. State on which lines and by which words there is
   evidence of:
   a) economic self-interest
   b) religious faith
   c) traditions in judicial practice
   d) belief in natural laws
   e) existing self-government in the colonies
   f) the idea of a constitution, even though the
      American Constitution was to be written
      eleven years later
   g) belief in the legitimacy of central government
   h) the idea of democratic government
   i) the fact that this is a revolutionary document
      and call to arms
   j) the feeling that Britain and America were
      separate entities
3. Name three types of primary sources that would
   help to confirm or deny the accusations made
   here against the "present King of Great Britain"
   and his co-conspirators.
4. Name two secondary works dealing with the
   Declaration.

b. This excerpt is from a speech by Prometheus, speaking to Io, in *Prometheus Bound* by Aeschylus:

1 Turn first toward the rising sun, and thitherward proceeding
2 over unplowed fields you will reach the nomad Scythians, a
3 people of mighty archers, who in their wicker-woven houses
4 dwelt aloft on smooth-rolling wagons. Approach not these,
5 but pass on through the land, keeping ever near to the surf-
6 beaten shores of the Euxine. To the left dwell the Chalybes,
7 famous workers of iron; and of them you must beware, for they
8 are a savage race and regard not strangers. Then will you
9 come to the River of Violence, fierce as its name and treach-
10 erous to ford; cross not over it until you have reached the
11 Caucasus, highest of mountains, where the river pours out its
12 fury over the brows of the cliffs. Here over the star-neigh-
13 boring summits you must toil and turn to the southern path; so
14 in time you will reach the host of the Amazons. . . . thou
15 wilt cross over the Maeotic strait, which ever after in memor-
16 ial of thy crossing men shall call the Bosporus, the fording
17 of the heifer. Thus thou wilt abandon the plain of Europe and
18 venture on the continent of Asia. [Translated by Paul Elmer
More, in Whitney T. Oates and Eugene O'Neill, Jr., eds., *The
Complete Greek Drama* (New York: Random House, 1938), vol.
1, pp. 147–148.]

1. What does the excerpt reveal, if anything, about
   (i) the Greek language, (ii) a translator's idea
   of what Greek oratory should sound like in
   English, (iii) the structure of the play?
2. Does the excerpt reveal anything about:
   a) civil engineering
   b) domestic architecture
   c) family and social organization
   d) religious belief
   e) technology and economics
   f) geography and topography
   g) transportation
   h) modes of conducting warfare
   i) agriculture and sources of power

        j) cultural anthropology

3. How would you go about placing a date on the play? Is there anything in the excerpted passage that would help, or anything within other parts of the play, or would you have to depend entirely on other sources?

4. If you wanted to get an idea of the place of this play in the total context of Greek drama or Greek culture, where would you look?

c. In writing a history, of course, a historian is not dependent upon one single source, but on many. If a single source must be scoured for all the meaning it may yield, several sources combined and related to each other will reveal more than any of them singly; the whole is greater than the sum of its parts. The following are two statements taken from the *New York Times* of September 26, 1962, and are sources (not the only ones) for an understanding of the "Meredith case," in which a Negro attempted to enroll in the University of Mississippi. In some respects these statements are similar; in others they are different; together they reveal things that neither statement reveals by itself. Statement A is an order of the United States Court of Appeals, Fifth Circuit (New Orleans), September 25, 1962:

1 It is ordered that the State of Mississippi, [Governor] Ross
2 R. Barnett [and others named], be temporarily restrained from
3 . . . 1. Arresting, attempting to arrest, prosecuting or
4 instituting any prosecution [against] . . . . 2. Instituting
5 or proceeding further in any civil action [against] . . . .
6 3. Injuring, harassing, threatening or intimidating James
7 Howard Meredith in any other way or by any other means on
8 account of his attending or seeking to attend the University
9 of Mississippi. . . .

Statement B is a proclamation by the Governor of Mississippi, also dated September 25, 1962:

1 I, Ross R. Barnett, Governor of the State of Mississippi,
2 having heretofore by proclamation, acting under the police
3 powers of the State of Mississippi, interposed the sovereignty
4 of this state on Sept. 14, 1962, and in order to prevent
5 violence and a breach of the peace, and in order to preserve
6 the peace, dignity and tranquillity of the State of Mississip-
7 pi, and having previously, on Sept. 20, 1962, denied to you,
8 James H. Meredith, admission to the University of Mississippi
9 under such proclamation and for such reasons, do hereby final-
10 ly deny you admission to the University of Mississippi.

1. In what respects are these two statements similar —i.e., what information do both of them reveal about the United States in the early 1960s (both, for example, obviously indicate that law is important)?
2. List several statements of probable significance that appear in Statement A, but not in Statement B; then several that appear in B, but not in A.
3. Would it have made any difference to Meredith, to the court, to the governor, or to a historian, which of the statements was made first?

3: HOMEWORK

a. The multiplicity of facts is immense. To get an idea of this multiplicity, try the following exercise. At the end of the day, choose a one-hour period during which you were awake; for example, 10:30 to 11:30 A.M. List as many facts or events as you can recall having happened to you during that period. If your memory and imagination are good, you will probably want to choose a much shorter period than an hour; James Joyce, in *Ulysses,* took nearly eight hundred pages to describe the events in the lives of a few people on a single day, June 16, 1904. Which of all these facts are the two or three most significant ones? Why do you choose them rather than others?

✓ *b.* Define, in ten words or less, each of the following terms: *fact, interpretation, generalization.*

SEVEN

EXPLAINING AND JUDGING THE PAST

1: BACKGROUND

FEW HISTORIANS TODAY would consider any mere listing of facts, any simple chronicle, to be "history." Adequate written history, the modern historian insists, must show relations between past events. The facts must "make sense" in some way. The very process of selecting the facts that "make sense" from the innumerable ones available requires a skillfully developed feedback process, as described in the preceding section. No sources, no history; but no judgment, no history, either. Judgment, truth, cause, and significance are all interconnected problems which lie at the root of historical explanation.

Here is an example of why this is so. If you were selecting a topic for a term paper, your instructor would probably consider it puerile and unsophisticated of you to say, "I want to write up the French Revolution," or "I'll do a history of the airplane." He would think so, at least, if he felt that by these topics you meant simply a collection of stray facts, to be strung together in chronological order. If, on the other hand, you were to examine a familiar subject from a fresh angle, as R. R. Palmer has done in *The Age of Democratic Revolution,* where he showed the common groundings of revolution in the seventeenth and late eighteenth centuries, including the English, French, and American, or if you could show how a piece of technology such as the airplane had great social consequences, such as the extension of warfare to large civilian populations by strategic bombing or the industrializing and urbanizing of rural areas because aircraft factories were built there, then you would be dealing with a mature historical problem—assuming that the sources were available. The historian, in short, must not only have his sources and the facts they reveal but must also have some notion of significance. This in itself takes judgment—to select a subject that is not banal, or boring, or inconsequential, or repetitive of existing written history. The achievement of truth is a further problem, since a pack of true facts do not make a true history. They have to be organized, related, thoroughly "fed back," and then hammered into a form that is convincing and communicable. The writing of history demands many thought processes and judgment above all. How do the facts relate? Are there any rules that can be followed when one tries to relate them? What do we mean by truth in history, and how can we identify it? Is there any sense in which the historian is a judge—Lord Acton (1834–1902) said he must be a "hanging judge"—of past events and people?

2: CAUSES IN HISTORY

HISTORIANS HAVE tended in recent years to avoid the term *cause,* for a variety of reasons, most important of which is the impossibility of explaining very definitely the actual relations and link-ups of causes and effects. But they have had great difficulty in avoiding it, and they often let it creep in through the back door disguised as "factors." What is undeniable is that some events bear some kind of relation to other events. What the relation consists of or how definite one can be about it is not very clear. The reason for this situation is rooted in the nature of history itself. In chemistry it is possible to say, "when we do this, then that will happen," and we can prove the cause-and-effect relation over and over again. In history things happen only once.

Somewhat similar things, which we can generalize about by sticking a label on them, such as wars, revolutions, social stratification, industrialism, and so forth, do happen more than once but never in quite the same way. Their contexts and circumstances are always a bit different, and because time runs in only one direction as far as human life is concerned, we can never test a historical hypothesis about cause and effect in the way that we could test a chemical one. For example, we can set up the hypothesis that the tax system of Louis XV and Louis XVI was a major cause of the French Revolution, but we cannot "run the experiment" once with that tax system operating and "run it through" a second time without that tax system, to see if the tax system makes any difference. We can, on the other hand, look at other apparently analogous upheavals such as the British "Glorious" Revolution of 1689, the American of 1776, and the Russian of 1917, as well as less successful ones such as the European upheavals of 1830 and 1848, the Taiping Rebellion in mid-nineteenth-century China, and the Russian revolution of 1905 and perhaps arrive at a decision as to whether governmental tax and revenue practices did or did not play some role in most of these cases. But we will never achieve the level of certainty that we can achieve in fifteen minutes in a chemical laboratory, because historical events happen only once.

When all is said and done, however, we cannot put aside the

idea that some past events shape later events, whether you wish to call those events "causes" or "factors" or whatever. To think otherwise would be to believe that history is completely chaotic and therefore meaningless and beyond any hope of rational reconstruction. We have to remember, however, that relationships in history are not only less certain than those in most physical sciences, but they are much more complex. A distinguished historian said recently that the worst thing one historian can call another historian today, aside from four-letter words, is a "monocausationist." In our daily lives it is obvious that any event depends on a great many other events; their interconnections are many, their causal relations complex. This complexity is compounded when we consider past events involving large numbers of people. For this reason, persons who like things black and white, who must ascribe a single overriding cause to an event, do not often make good historians. The past is messy and no clearer than a forest in a fog. This is why historically minded persons sometimes say, to the disbelief of scientists, that the natural sciences are relatively "simple" compared to history. While causal relationships in natural science are relatively clear and uncomplicated, such relationships in human affairs, past or present, are extremely complicated and, what is more, not easy to prove with certainty one way or the other.

Lack of complete certainty and the presence of great complexity are therefore the basic characteristics of historical relationships. Historical causation is both more complicated and less definite than scientific causation. But this is hardly to say that historical causation is completely uncertain and completely chaotic. You can see this for yourself if you consider the following questions:

  a. Put your mind to some event you have been studying recently: the defeat of the Spanish Armada in 1588, German and Allied strategy and tactics in 1914–

1915, or one of the American presidential elections, for example. These are all events of a political or military character. Can you ascribe one single cause to your event? Do you see a number of causes having been involved? Try separating the several causes you probably find into "remote" causes and "proximate" causes; the distinction between these two types may be fuzzy in places, but in many instances it will help to give order to your scheme of causes. How certain can you be of the effect of any one of your causes? Does it seem that all of the causes put together carry more certainty than any one of them alone?

b. Put your mind now to some event such as the fall of the Roman Empire, the Enlightenment, the impact of industrialization on east Asia, or urbanization in America—an event of a social, economic, or intellectual character. Ask the same questions as before. Any results? Although the problem of causal ascription will probably seem to you to get worse, are your results *completely* uncertain? Perhaps you will agree with the proposition that certainty and complexity work in inverse proportion with regard to historical events—the more complex, the less certain; the more certain, the less complex.

3: LAWS IN HISTORY

THE PROBLEMS OF causation would, of course, be made much easier if definite laws existed in human affairs, governing all events, just as the law of conservation of energy and the law of gravity exist in physical science. Fifty years ago, probably, the majority of historians believed that laws existed in history, though few of these laws, if any, had been discovered since "scientific" history had begun, three-quarters of a century earlier. Today historians, at least in the Western world, seldom put much stock in historical laws. Some philosophers maintain that there are indeed "covering laws," which are really generalizations about how people must react in certain types of situations; a controversy continues over the existence of "covering laws," but historians point out that none seem to be identifiable even if they do exist. Certain historians, most prominently the Marxians, maintain that there are stages of development through which human societies, undergoing class struggle, must inevitably pass. But many other historians, today the majority, seem to agree that universally operative laws are bound to drown in the swirling sea of time. Time, of course, is essential to history. Without time, everything would remain the same, and it would be impossible to trace the development of anything. On the other hand, everything that passes through time is subject to change; if "historical laws" are generalizations about changing events, it follows that the laws themselves must change as events change. This does not mean that long-term historical generalizations are impossible or even imprudent to make, but that they cannot have the certainty that ordinarily attaches to a scientific or theological law. Can you think of anything that does not change, even though it may change very slowly? Does anything exist outside of time?

4: TRUTH IN HISTORY

THE IDENTIFICATION of truthfulness in a work of history is, of course, a specialized aspect of the problem of locating truthfulness in anything, and one's acceptance of a historical work as truthful will depend on how one identifies truth in general. In the next chapter we will look at what philosophers call the "coherence theory of truth" and the "correspondence theory of truth," and this is not the place to try to decide between the rival claims of those two metaphysical positions. Both of them revolve around a further philosophical question, the nature of perception—whether we perceive the outside world directly and accurately or, on the other hand, only approximately, through the cloud of our own culture, experience, and preconceptions. The whole general problem of perception and truth is doubly vexatious in the case of history and writings about history, since, as we have seen, we can never look directly at the things we are thinking or writing about in history but necessarily have to view them through the medium of the sources. The sources, since they are often incomplete and in some way distorted, make the truth, whatever it may be, even less easy to perceive with regard to the past than direct eye-witness perception makes it with regard to the present. We should remind ourselves, however, before we consign the search for truth in history to the realm of the hopeless, that direct perceptions of the present are often incomplete and distorted too. This is especially true of large events or trends, which we may live through but of which we can experience only a small part directly; a worm's-eye view is not by any means the best view. In judging truthfulness, past or present, we are still thrown back on the trustworthiness that we decide we should attach to perception.

On the purely factual level of truth, of course, there is not much argument. If anyone states that Nero was pope instead of emperor, that Bismarck led the unification of Italy rather than of Germany, or that the War of 1812 began in 1822, he says what is not true. One can argue at great length and travel many semantic byways in pursuit of just why these statements are untrue or in what possible senses they might be true, but from any operational viewpoint they are undoubtedly false because they do not square with any universally accepted chronological and institutional frameworks. In the ordinary and universally accepted senses of the terms *emperor, Germany,* and *1812,* these terms relate to Nero, Bismarck, and the scuffle the Americans had with Britain in the early nineteenth century; the terms *pope, Italy,* and *1822* just do not fit. Factual truth is not always so easily established or universally accepted, but when it is, truth is clear enough.

The going gets more difficult when generalization and interpretation are involved. At first sight it may seem surprising, but it is entirely possible in a work of history (or a present-day newspaper article or an eyewitness account) to be correct at every factual point but thoroughly incorrect in the overall account. Some facts may have been left out that would change the story essentially; some facts may be in the wrong order; some may have received the wrong stress. This takes us back to the inevitability of generalization and interpretation, and the principle that facts, although they are absolutely necessary in the writing of history, really mean practically nothing unless they can be related to each other by a conscious mind with good judgment.

But how do we judge "good judgment"? How do we identify "truthful history" even after we determine that the history in question is truthful on the purely factual level?

The following statements suggest alternative answers to these questions. In class discussion, choose and be prepared to defend the one you think makes most sense. If none does, draw up one of your own.

1. The history in question is persuasive; it convinces us, just as a well-written novel convinces us, of its essential truth.

2. The history in question follows closely the interpretation and ordering of facts that we can find in an original source. For example, if we find that an account of the founding of Rome follows Livy or that an ac-

count of World War II follows General Eisenhower's memoirs, it must be true.

3. The history in question does not go to any extremes. It is moderate in tone, seems factual and unbiased, and lacks a strong point of view that the author seems intent on foisting on us.

4. The history in question definitely and unmistakably states what the author finds as having happened. There is no argument about it.

5. The history in question seems to correspond to the facts. No more need be asked.

6. The history in question seems to correspond to what we know of the period under discussion, and it also corresponds to our experience of how people behave.

7. The history in question fits known laws of history.

5: JUDGMENT IN HISTORY

HISTORIANS MUST make many kinds of judgments in the exercise of their craft, and these range from the very practical to the very abstract. One category of judgments has already been touched upon: the technical judgments required for the evaluation of sources. Is a source what it purports to be? Is it credible, and if so to what degree; what is it worth? How does this fact relate to these other facts? Another category of judgments is also a matter of craft and may be called logistical. Once a historian has come upon a problem in the past that he thinks is worth researching and writing about—a decision that requires considerable judgment in itself —he has to ask himself the very practical and logistical questions of how feasible the problem is as a research project. Are the sources available? Do they exist? Will whoever keeps them make them available for research? How much time will it take to visit the archives and libraries where the sources are, and how are the research trips to be financed? How long will the whole project take, and is it really worth the time and effort? Any experienced historian finds first-rate research topics that he cannot undertake because one or more of these practical problems cannot be resolved satisfactorily. If a key group of sources has been destroyed by fire, if a family owns certain key papers and won't permit them to be examined, if a key body of papers is in Albania and an American passport is not valid for Albania, if the sources are widely scattered around the United States and time or travel money is not to be had, the historian must decide that the project is not the right one for him.

He must also make other, more abstract judgments. Historians often speak of "historical judgments" and "moral judgments," both of which relate to the ways the historian regards his sources and how he derives meaning from them. Nearly all historians accept the necessity of making "historical" judgments, but most of them try to avoid "moral" judgments. The distinction is not perfect, but it is fairly clear. Let us say a certain man holding a political office—and he may be an ancient Roman or a modern German or a modern American—imprisons several thousand citizens or residents of his country. The sources state this unmistakably, and they also indicate that the politician took that action because he felt it was necessary in order to preserve the domestic tranquillity of the country. The sources may also suggest that the politician, like many or most of his countrymen at the time, sincerely believed that the people he imprisoned were intrinsically dangerous. For the Roman in the second century A.D., the people happened to be Christians. For the German in 1940, they were Jews. For the twentieth-century American, they were American citizens of Japanese descent during World War II. What is the historian to make of these events? How is he to judge the politician?

He has got to decide, and it is not easy to do so, whether the politician's action was based on a real and known danger to the state, whether his ideology and perceptions bound him to take such an action and to what extent he was really influenced by that ideology, whether his action was quite idiosyncratic or was fairly normal considering the culture and institutions of his time, and, aside from such questions of motivation, whether the politician's action achieved the purposes it was intended to and what side effects it had. These are all generally within the category of "historical" judgments, as are a number of other judgments that the historian will probably need or want to make.

On the other hand, he may believe firmly that the imprisonment of people without redress or due process of law is morally wrong and that any action or ideology that tends toward such deprivation of personal liberty must be condemned. He may find in the sources the suggestion that the politician took such action in the hope of personal advancement or financial gain, and the historian, therefore, might consider the politician morally corrupt for having placed his own personal benefit above the freedom of so many other persons. If, as happened to the Christians in Rome and to the Jews in Germany, they were not only imprisoned but slaughtered, the historian may condemn such mass murder on what most of us today would consider obvious moral grounds. Generally speaking, a moral judgment rests on some principle that the historian and, perhaps, his society believes and holds; a historical judgment rests, as a rule, on a collection of data about how people behave in certain circumstances and how their actions, motivations aside, have effects.

All of this raises questions for discussion. Is it the historian's job to make judgments, either historical (e.g., John of England was an incompetent ruler, or President Grant was an incompetent president) or moral (e.g., King John or President Grant were morally corrupt, either through venality or laxity)? If the historian does make such judgments, is he not applying his own "laws," biases, or "frame of reference" (the way he looks out at the world, because his experience is of a particular time and place) to a time and place in which things were different and therefore were subject to different "frames of reference," and about which it would be grossly unfair to require conformity with the "frame of reference" of a later age? If the historian does not make such judgments, is he not lacking in forthrightness and courage, not to say usefulness to his readers? To what extent should a historian place himself within the "frame of reference" of the place, time, and persons in the past about which he is writing? To what extent will he be able to?

6: HOMEWORK

    a. Define *law, truth,* and *explanation,* as used in history, in ten words or less for each.

    b. Distinguish between historical and moral judgment by means of a concrete example drawn from your course material.

    c. Demonstrate the "logistical judgment" required of historians by selecting a research problem and deciding (i) whether sources are available, (ii) how you might get to them, (iii) how long the project will take, and (iv) whether it is worth doing in terms of the contribution it would make to scholarship.

7: DIGGING

THE FOLLOWING ARE a few of the outstanding discussions of problems raised in this section.

Beale, Howard K. "What Historians Have Said about the Causes of the Civil War," in Bulletin 54, *Theory and Practice in Historical Study*. New York: Social Science Research Council, 1946. Pages 53–102. A revealing analysis of the great difficulty historians have had in assessing the causes of a great event and, by implication, a discussion of the concept of historical cause.

Benson, Lee. *Toward the Scientific Study of History*. Philadelphia: J. B. Lippincott Company, 1972. See especially Chapter 8, "Explanations of American Civil War Causation: A Critical Assessment and a Modest Proposal to Reorient and Reorganize the Social Sciences." A pointed and up-to-date argument for methodological rigor.

Dray, William H. *Laws and Explanation in History*. New York: Oxford University Press, 1957. A difficult philosophical analysis of the problems of laws in history but a very rewarding one.

Smith, Page. *The Historian and History*. New York: Alfred A. Knopf, 1964. Chapter 11 deals with the problem of interpreting the American Revolution and with how little the vaunted perspective of time assists the historian. Engagingly written, as is the rest of Smith's book.

Walsh, W. H. *Philosophy of History: An Introduction*. New York: Harper and Brothers, 1960. Especially Chapter 4, which discusses theories of truth.

EIGHT

WHEN EXPERTS DISAGREE
(OR, CAN HISTORY
BE OBJECTIVE?)

1: BACKGROUND

A RECURRING PROBLEM in history, as in nearly everything
else, is the trustworthiness, lack of bias, and plain truthfulness of a historical work. The question arises very frequently,
is this objective? Is one book on a subject more objective than
another one? The problem is seldom resolved, partly because
objectivity and truth are much harder to identify and define
than they seem to be at first glance. Philosophers often distinguish between a "correspondence" theory of truth (a thing
is true if it corresponds to what is known to be true) and a "coherence" theory of truth (a thing is true if it is self-consistent,
i.e., if it hangs together plausibly). But the former theory still
leaves open the question of how one tells whether something
corresponds to the truth if the truth is not known for certain,
as it often isn't; and the latter theory leaves unanswered the
problem that that which is coherent or plausible to one person,
say an Indian peasant, may not be so to another person, such
as a Swiss banker.

To add to this philosophical difficulty about the identifiability of truth itself, history poses special problems, resulting particularly from the fact that history must be dealt with at second hand; what is past can be known only through records left from the past and cannot be known directly. The degree to which objective knowledge, truthful or certain knowledge, can be had of the historical past has been a matter of some disagreement among historians. A certain school of them, which represented the generally held view in the nineteenth century but is much less widespread today, has believed that the documents explain themselves and need only to be verified —i.e., proved to be what they purport to be—and arranged in proper and self-evident order. This process will reveal the past "as it actually happened," as Leopold von Ranke phrased it so famously. This kind of history was often called "scientific history."

Another view, elaborated effectively for the first time by the German philosopher of history Wilhelm Dilthey (1833–1911) agreed with the Rankeans that history was a definite body of reality outside the investigator, which the investigator therefore approached as an object apart from himself. But the history written by one investigator would unavoidably differ from a history written by someone else whose experiences had been different, since a historian could not possibly understand past events without reference to events, realities, and relationships that he had personally experienced. History, in this view, would have to be relative to the historian. But, in this view, history still had for its subject matter a definite segment of reality, an unchangeable and unchanging object. Because of these two elements—the objective nature of what is studied and the relativity of outlook among those who study it—this school of thought has been called "objective relativism" and has been adopted by a great many historians in the twentieth century. Few of them got the idea directly from Dilthey, and usually absorbed it from later theorists, both European and American, and from each other as it grew more popular. But whatever its roots in a particular case, "objective relativism" describes the general outlook of the mass of historians today, at least in the United States.

Still a third school of thought, differing from the "history as it actually happened" view and from "objective relativism" as well, denies that the past exists any longer as an objective entity, but must inevitably be the creation of the historian's mind. The significant events of the past—revolutions, social changes, ideological developments—were too vast to have been understood when they were taking place, and they came into existence only when a modern historian created them. This view was adopted in the early twentieth century by a portion of the historical profession, and its most notable exponent in America was Carl Becker (1873–1945), at least at certain times during Becker's life. Because of its denial that there is such a thing as a self-existing past for historians to write about, and since it makes history depend completely on the historian, this view has been called "subjective relativism." Many historians have never been very happy with subjective relativism because it seems to take very little account of the records that have survived, partial and confusing though they may be. The sources, however, cannot be denied: one cannot say that Columbus made his first voyage to the New World in 1392 or 1592 any more than one can say that $2 + 2 = 5$. Subjective relativism, in many people's view, does not make an adequate distinction between history and pure fiction. Still, and here the subjective and objective relativists would generally agree, the historical understanding of large and long-term events, such as the rise of modern nationalism, the social effects of industrialization, the growth of cities in ancient and modern times, unquestionably requires a conscious mind, and that mind will inevitably differ from another conscious mind in how it understands those events. Different minds build different models. There are presently some signs that relativism is waning; a number of historians will now contend that what Becker called "the historian's climate of opinion," or subjective frame of reference, does not affect his understanding of problems of at least limited scope—and that research and recapitulation of these problems is basically replicable. The heyday of relativism is undoubtedly over. But the relativist approach, in modified form, remains common, partly for the following (historical) reasons.

The shift from the old "history as it actually happened" way of looking at things to one or another kind of relativism is itself an interesting chapter in the history of ideas. Only one of these reasons need be mentioned here, because it indicates something about the different characteristics of different kinds of history. Much of the history written in the nineteenth century and a good part of what is written today deal with fairly concrete, visible events which are clearly evident in the sources and which actually do resolve themselves into a narrative without much argument about what these facts mean. This is especially true of political and diplomatic history, most of all when the question at hand is a rather short-term one such as a particular administrative policy, a particular war, or the foreign relations of one country with certain other countries over a limited time-span. On the other hand, long-term events with complex consequences are very often not clearly and consecutively apparent in the sources. Since a greater and greater percentage of historical work concerns such subjects, it is not surprising that historians' attitudes toward the objectivity of their task are changing too.

The difference between the two kinds of history is evident in examples such as the French Revolution or the American Civil War. The political and military facts about these events are rather well established; there are many narratives that set forth "the way they all happened," and this kind of history does not need much rewriting. What Mirabeau, Louis XVI, and the people of Paris did on certain days in 1789 and after or how Lincoln, Grant, Lee, and the Union and Confederate armies behaved between early 1861 and early 1865 are for the most part pretty definitely known. But if a historian asks what long-range effect the French Revolution had on France and the rest of Western Europe for the next century, or for that matter *why* Mirabeau acted as he did, or what the Parisian class structure was in 1789, or whether American development was influenced significantly by the Civil War and in what ways, he is dealing with a problem of a quite different order. The relevant facts are not going to be as obvious; his answers are not going to be as definite, and his belief in the "objectivity" of his task is not going to be as strong as it will be in the case of the historian who deals with the concrete, visible narrative. Both kinds of history are necessary, but the differences between them understandably lead to differences of opinion about whether history is "objective." It seems, in short, that some historians are more objective than others, depending on what kind of history they're writing.

2: FEEDBACK

SOME OF THE problems relating to "objectivity" in history should become vivid in discussions of the following questions.

> *a. The term* objectivity. We use the term frequently: Is this book or that newspaper "objective"? What do we mean by the term? Which of the following words is the antonym of *objective: subjective, relative,* or *wrong*?
>
> *b. The "whole truth."* Everyone interested in American history agrees that the Civil War was highly significant

for future American development. Everyone interested in the history of Western civilization or of the world agrees that the French Revolution had consequences that were sweeping and profound. Many historians have written about the events leading up to the Civil War or to the French Revolution, about the war and revolution themselves, and about what differences they made to future generations. But if you asked these historians why, in the last analysis, these cataclysmic events came about and why they made any difference, few of them will agree, and probably no two of them will agree completely. In the case of the Civil War, some lay the affair to an inevitable conflict of two radically different cultures; some say the basic disagreement was economic; some say the two sides simply stopped listening and trying to understand each other; some say it was an argument over the interpretation of the Constitution; others advance other reasons. There is very little disagreement about the "facts," such as the terms of the Compromise of 1850, or the authorship of the Kansas-Nebraska bill, or the state of the international cotton market, or what was said in the Lincoln-Douglas debates, or the voting in the election of 1860, or the frantic attempts to halt secession during the winter of 1860–61. There is not even much disagreement about whether these and other "facts" were significant, more or less.

What varies among historians is (i) which facts, among thousands, were most significant and (ii) how these facts should fit together to form a coherent explanation. The question is, are all of these historians wrong? Are all of them partially right? Are all, none, or some of them "objective"? The same questions can be asked of the historians who have attempted to come to grips with the French Revolution. Was it class struggle, internal weaknesses within the French government, the failure of the monarch to act efficiently and decisively, the ideas of the Enlightenment corroding the institutions of monarchic and ecclesiastical authority, a scarcity of bread, or other reasons that precipitated the conflict? How should one arrange all the trends and events—the facts, long-range and short-range—that undeniably contributed to the revolution?

  c. *Objectivity and moderation.* Students of history, when confronted with a spectrum of interpretations of a major problem like the Civil War or the French Revolution, sometimes gain the impression that objectivity does not exist or that it consists simply of the middlemost or least controversial position among the many offered.

    1. Would, in fact, an "objective" account of the causes of the Civil War or of the French Revolution be one that included parts of all the existing and varying accounts?

    2. Would it be one that took the "most moderate" point of view between the "extremes" of existing accounts?

    3. Would sources have anything to do with establishing an answer to this problem?

    4. Would it be possible to have a single, "objective" account of the French Revolution or the American Civil War?

  d. *Are all histories created equal?* If several historians writing about the same event produce varying histories of it—in other words, if the experts seem to disagree—some might think that one man's history is as good (or bad) as another's. We will reject this as false; if it were not false, it would be pointless to study history at all, since the opinion of a beginner would be as good as that of a seasoned scholar, and a novel would do as well as a well-researched historical account. One would have no need for facts or sources, and history could be written like poetry. Now if we grant that everyone is entitled to his own opinion or his own history, must we say that every history is equally truthful or valid? If we assume that two historical accounts of some event are not equally valid or invalid, how can we tell which is the better one? What makes some histories better than others? Is there a measure of objectivity or something like it after all? On the other hand, is it possible that two different explanations of the same event could both be true, or at least of some help in getting at the truth?

You are confronted here with a serious and difficult question which involves most of what has been discussed earlier. It may be that historians can, should, but have not yet, evolved devices for thoroughly measuring objectivity and truth. But they have undeniably done so to a considerable degree— again, the less complex, the more certain.

3: DIGGING

THE HISTORICAL PROFESSION in America, since its beginnings about a century ago, has encompassed a number of points of view, even among the presidents of the American Historical Association, with regard to "objectivity." The leading views were expressed in the space of about a decade in the presidential addresses of Edward P. Cheyney (1923), Carl L. Becker (1931), and Charles A. Beard (1934). Cheyney represented the "as it actually happened" or "scientific" school; Becker represented "subjective relativism," and Beard "objective relativism." These labels oversimplify the positions of the three men, but their addresses do represent broadly how the three schools of thought took shape in the writing of thoughtful men. The three addresses are worth reading, and may be found in the January issues of the *American Historical Review* for 1924, 1932, and 1935, respectively.

Page Smith, in *The Historian and History,* Chapter 13, makes a distinction between what he calls "existential history" and "symbolic history," which is somewhat like the distinction discussed above between the histories of the concrete, visible event and the histories of the long-term, complex event. Smith is very clear and helpful on this point.

Another excellent discussion is in Chapter 7 of Arthur Danto's *Analytical Philosophy of History* (Cambridge: At the University Press, 1965). Danto dismisses Beard's complaint that a "perfect" knowledge of the past is impossible; Danto asks, why would that even be desirable, any more than a picture should become the thing it represents? A degree of subjectivity is "inexpungeable," but, he implies, need not be as great as many relativists maintain.

4: HOMEWORK

    a. State two reasons for and two reasons against the contention that a history textbook is "objective."

    b. Define in ten words or less *objective relativism, subjective relativism,* and *scientific history.*

NINE

WORKABLE TOPICS: THE MAN ON THE STREET AND HOW TO SET HIM STRAIGHT

1: BACKGROUND

FEW THINGS ARE more common in speech or writing today than appeals to the historical past. We have become accustomed to a world that changes and develops, and consequently we are more aware of the "historicity"—the changeableness of people and things over a time-span—than mankind has generally been until very recent times. The historical way of looking at things is almost exclusively a twentieth-century phenomenon, despite the fact that men have been on earth for a long time. It is now the normal thing when statesmen or other public men wish to present a rationale for some action or when persons of almost any level of education want to find support for their beliefs to claim that "history" backs them up and that their belief or action was formulated with the "lessons of history" in mind.

People often do not realize that they habitually think in historical terms and use historical arguments. They may use history crudely, but use it they do to create a past that provides a backdrop consistent with what they presently believe or wish to do. Historians regard this respect for history with mixed feelings. On the one hand, they are flattered and consoled because of the respectful attention people give to history, but on the other hand they are horrified by the crudeness and unthinking dogmatism, not to say presumptuousness, with which the appeals to the past are often made.

The following statements are, change a word or two, of the sort that one is apt to hear or read almost anytime. Each of them is really a historical generalization which, if taken literally, would commit the person who used it to a staggering command of knowledge about the past. The first few are particularly common and particularly roughhewn, and they represent an expert historical judgment about as closely as a statement that toads cause warts represents medical science. People who make such statements would not think of attempting open-heart surgery or defending a client in court on a felony charge, but rendering historical judgments on matters of extreme complexity is all in a day's work. These are some statements that one hears more or less frequently:

1. Things aren't what they used to be.

2. This great country is moving ahead faster than ever before.

3. Turmoil and crisis are everywhere today. Our very survival is constantly in danger. Oh, for the good old days when things were tranquil, people were happy, and the world was at peace.

4. Our moral standards—especially those relating to courtship and marriage—are going downhill fast. We are getting soft and corrupt, and our only salvation lies in a return to the sober morality of our forefathers.

5. The people of the world are moving inevitably toward a better standard of living (or nuclear destruction, or class struggle).

6. War is inevitable within the next few years. Arms races always lead to wars, and the present arms race is the biggest ever.

7. History proves that revolutionary movements spring from poverty and other social conditions which enrage the depressed masses.

8. Revolutions, no matter how radical at the beginning, always are followed by a "Thermidor," a period of reaction. Eventually the radical and reactionary elements fuse into a new status quo.

9. The Republican party, like the Democratic party a few decades earlier, started as a liberal movement but soon became conservative.

10. Republicans always bring depressions, and Democrats always bring wars.

2: FEEDBACK

THESE STATEMENTS NEED some discussion. Consider these general criticisms of the ten statements:

   a. Are any of the ten statements, in whole or in part, suitable in their present form for historical analysis? Select one of the first five and one of the second five. Can these statements be proved or disproved, as they now stand? Can you think of obvious exceptions to them? (Example: Statement 2 is really an assertion about growth rates, that they are higher now than at some time or all times in the past. Before you could deal with this, you would have to decide which rates, of those available, are the key ones; what are the indices of significant growth; how sure of them you can be; etc.)

   b. As topics for historical investigation, why do they require amendment or even total discarding? Here are some possible faults; where do they appear in the statements?

1) Presuppositions, such as a faith in progress, that are not easily subjected to proof
2) Questionable theses, e.g., that "things were tranquil" in the past
3) Imprecise meaning, especially of nouns
4) Overgeneralization
5) The sources needed to confirm or deny the statement are unavailable
6) The sources needed to confirm or deny the statement are too vast or too scattered
7) The statement contains an unscientific hypothesis, which is extremely difficult to prove or disprove (e.g., the Freudian hypothesis that human motivation is sexually based).

3: HOMEWORK

CHOOSE ONE OF the first five statements. Then:

a. Rephrase it, either as a single statement or as several statements, if necessary, so as to include as much as possible of its content, yet to make it more susceptible of proof or disproof. (Try putting your revised statements in the form of questions. It helps to think of historical analysis as interrogation and cross-examination of the sources.)

b. What fields of history and what other disciplines may be involved in the process of proving or disproving the statement? In other words, what areas would one presumably have to be familiar with in order to investigate thoroughly the problem raised by the statement?

    c. List three sources, either primary or secondary, in your library which would help you prove or disprove your problem. State in a short phrase how each source would help.

    d. Assume that you are going to write a book to prove or disprove your problem. Give a very brief (half-page) outline of your book.

       Do the same things with one of the statements numbered from six through ten.

TEN

LANGUAGE, THE VEHICLE OF HISTORY

1: BACKGROUND

HISTORY, UNLIKE MANY of the sciences, is intimately bound up with language. If we must say, "no sources, no history," and "no thought, no history," we must also say, "no literacy, no history." This dependence upon language is one of the things that makes history so enjoyable but at the same time so annoying. Without fluency, accuracy, and a sense of organization in language, a person can never become a good historian, regardless of his diligence, skill, or judgment in other ways. The very processes of historical synthesis and interpretation simply cannot exist unless they take place in the form of written or spoken language. This means that the more skillful a person is as a writer or a speaker, the more likely it is that he will be good at history. But it means more than this; it means also that his analysis and conclusions will be only as good as his language skill, only as exact as his language facility. He will be prone not only to historical errors but to errors of language as well. History faces not only its own inherent limits, such as a lack of sources or the great difficulty involved in finding out what motivated certain people to do certain things, but it must contend also with the limits of language. Historical conclusions never have the apparent exactness of mathematical ones, and even basic terms—the labeling generalizations we have already talked about—tend to be imprecise. An x^2 is always an x^2, but is a liberal always a liberal, a slave always a slave, one republic just like another republic? Seldom.

Leaving aside for the moment the problems connected with the proper use of grammar, organization, and word meaning, which are common to anything that appears in the form of written language, we should look at the linguistic problems that particularly beset historians. If you are perceptive, you will see that most of these problems are linguistic aspects of the problem of historical generalization. How can a "labeling generalization" derived from one culture or set of events properly be applied to another culture or set of events? How can terms which derive from events in one time period be properly applied to other time periods, especially earlier ones? Couldn't the whole problem of linguistic imprecision as regards labeling generalizations be avoided by the use of symbols, as in mathematics? The following discussion topics should bring out some of the problems and possibilities involved in answering these questions.

2: FEEDBACK

a. *The tyranny of terms.* Among the multitude of people who have been called "liberals" are Socrates, Jesus, Gautama Buddha, John Locke, Mazzini, Thomas Jefferson, Gandhi, and Harry S. Truman. An equally diverse group, such as Cato the Censor, Bismarck, the Emperor Charles V, Czar Nicholas II, Alexander

Hamilton, Winston Churchill, and Barry Goldwater, have been dubbed "conservative."

1. Is there any consistent meaning to the terms *liberal* and *conservative* as applied to these two groups? Do the diversities outweigh the similarities?
2. Do you think the terms are so varied in meaning as to be useless? Should they be discarded from the historical vocabulary?
3. How might the imprecision that these terms exemplify be overcome?

b. *Cross-cultural labeling. Liberal* and *conservative* are applied to widely different kinds of people. So are other terms originally derived from the relating to certain times, places, and cultures; for example, the terms *slavery, feudalism, frontier, industry, urbanism, middle class.*

1. Use each of these terms in a number of contexts to demonstrate how they may be applied to different regions, cultures, and time periods.
2. Are the differences in such usages greater or less than the similarities?
3. Do these terms, applied in so many ways, help us to understand the things they refer to, or do they blur essential differences?

c. *Anachronism.* This is a fault in writing. It means the application of a term to a different time, especially an earlier time, than that to which it properly belongs. An anachronism can be simply a matter of carelessness or sloppy writing. But it may also reflect a deeper problem—essentially that of inappropriate generalization, the failure on the part of the writer to get back fully into the complexities of the period he is talking about and to separate the events or structures of that period from those of the present—for example, the use of *democracy* with reference to eighteenth-century England, or *nationalism* with reference to medieval Italy, where in neither case do those terms apply in anything like the sense in which we commonly use them now. There are anachronisms among these statements.

1. In the decades following the "Glorious Revolution" England moved toward democratic government.
2. It was the Roman *haute bourgeoisie* and their domestics who suffered most heavily from the rain of volcanic ash upon Pompeii.
3. The American Revolution was, in a sense, an uprising aimed at the destruction of feudalism.
4. Italian nationalism plagued both pope and emperor in the eleventh and twelfth centuries.

Now, where are the anachronisms in these sentences? What else, by the way, is wrong with any of them? Is there a difference between anachronism and inappropriate metaphor? (E.g., in 4: *nationalism* is anachronistic; *plagued* is metaphorical.) How could the sentences be rephrased to avoid the anachronisms as well as other improprieties?

d. *Would symbols help?* If language makes history imprecise, perhaps symbols could be substituted for words, as is done to an extent in mathematics and in symbolic logic. Would this help to remove the imprecision that language seems to force upon history? If not, why not? What is the difference, if anything, between a word and a symbol as means of describing events or persons?

e. *Time changes in word meanings.* Another problem in historical research is that the meaning of a word may change over time. For example, the terms *science* and *law* meant different things to the educated person of the mid-nineteenth century than they mean to us. You may think of some other examples.

3: DIGGING

TWO GOOD DEMONSTRATIONS of that recurrent historical problem, the use of a word derived from one culture or time to describe events in another culture or time, may be found with reference to Chinese and to ancient Greek history in the book edited by Louis Gottschalk, *Generalization in the Writing of History* (Chicago: University of Chicago Press, 1963). They are:

Finley, M. I. "Generalizations in Ancient History," pp. 19–35 in the Gottschalk book. Why it is not accurate to apply the modern term *slave* to ancient Greece. An example of the difficulties inherent in cross-cultural labeling, as well as an example of anchronism.

Wright, Arthur F. "On the Uses of Generalization in the Study of Chinese History," pp. 36–58; see also Derk Bodde, "Comments on the Paper of Arthur F. Wright," pp. 59–65. An example of cross-cultural labeling: why it is imprecise to apply the western term *feudalism* to Chinese civilization.

4: HOMEWORK

SOME FURTHER EXERCISES which should help you think through the problems discussed in this section:

    a. List some times and cultures to which the terms *industry* or *industrial* have been applied. Is the term constant in its meaning, or are there variations depending on its application?

b. Look through one of the chapters of your text, and see if you can locate any examples of anachronism.

c. What differences are there among "aristocrats" of England, the Soviet Union, the United States, and Argentina?

ELEVEN

EVERYMAN HIS
OWN COPY EDITOR

1: BACKGROUND

IN THE PRECEDING section there appeared some basic problems that recur when the historian attempts to cast his thoughts, as he must, in words and sentences. Those problems were found to be inherent in the nature of historical generalization and synthesis. This section is also concerned with history and language, but in more general terms. Now we want to know what a decent historical essay looks like. Such an essay must be accurate in its historical facts, sensible in its relating of them, well organized, and without grammatical errors or misspellings. What follows is a series of historical essays which might have been answers on college history examinations but which are not of the quality that they might be. Revise them in discussion or on paper.

2: FEEDBACK

   a. Early American and early modern European history.

This is a transcript of an answer received on a freshman examination paper to the question, "State and discuss the conditions prevailing in England that led to colonization in North America in the early seventeenth century." (Grade received: F)

1 Mainly because of a need for relgious freedoms and a frustra-
2 tion coming from the people the migration occurred.
3 But their were underlieing reasons also, the growing hatred
4 for church and state—the resentment of the people against
5 jailing advocates of free thought—the high prices and low
6 wages—so a promise of a new free rights and fertil land
7 cought the attention of many of the English—and they go—

Questions:
1. Which of the following faults of English composition occur in the passage, and where? (i) split infinitive, (ii) comma splice, (iii) poor sentence structure, (iv) poor paragraph organization, (v) improper capitalization, (vi) dangling participle, (vii) failure of agreement of person, case, tense, or number
2. Note each misspelled word in the passage and spell it properly.
3. Which of the following faults of historical narration occur in the passage and where? (i) error of fact, (ii) questionable interpretation, (iii) incompleteness of causal explanation, (iv) unsupported generalization, (v) anachronism in idea (reading the present back into the past)
   b. *Recent American history*. The following is an answer also from a freshman examination paper. The question was "Compare and contrast American economic

life of the 1920s with that of the 1950s." (Grade received: F)

1 In the 20s the Presidents were Harding, A Republican, and
2 Hoover, a Democrat. To really make the economy go,
3 along the desired lines of lassie fair, there was Henry Ford and
4 his Model t and A, the Wright Brothers, and J. P. Morgan.
5 Theodore Roosevelt was dead by then. The farmers did not
6 share in the prosperity. The flappers did very often. Therefore
7 when the Crash came in 29 it really hit, and man I mean really.
8 Hoover tries to bring in the New Deal to make things go, but
9 didn't. In the 50s things evened out more.

Questions:

1. Which of the following grammatical faults occur in the passage, and where? (i) split infinitive, (ii) failure of agreement of person, case, or number, (iii) improper verb form, (iv) improper punctuation, (v) improper capitalization, (vi) poor sentence structure

2. Note each misspelled word and spell it correctly.

3. In which of the following ways is the passage inadequate as an essay or as an answer to the question asked? State where each of these faults occurs. (i) excess verbiage, (ii) irrelevant information, (iii) pointless wit, (iv) lack of paragraph organization, (v) general imbalance as an answer to the question

4. In which of the following ways is the passage inadequate as written history? State where each occurs. (i) error of fact, (ii) questionable interpretation, (iii) lack of definition of terms, (iv) illogical narration, (v) inadequate or improper causal explanation, (vi) significant omissions of fact or generalization

c. *History of civilization, early.* The following is a dis-
astrous answer to the examination question, "Give a
précis of the main reasons for the fall of the Roman
Empire in the West." What grade would you assign it?

1 It is not easy to say why the roman Empire finally disappeared
2 because it took so long and there was so much of it. Disease,
3 money, leadership, the legalation of Christianity, and outside
4 forces all had apart. Even such great Romans as Diocletian,
5 Constantine, and Theoderic could do little. By the time Jus-
6 tinian and his gothic hordes knocked off the last emporer,
7 Romulus, Augustulus, in 476, there was not much to knock off.
8 "The glory that was Greece, the grandeur that was Rome" was
9 pretty tarnished anyway. The machinations of the Empress
10 Galla Placidia and other corrupt villeins weakened the empire
11 from the inside. Barbarians were moving in from the outside.
12 Traitors to Rome like Julian the Apostle hurt greatly. People
13 who had been living in luxury for 400 years had no steam left
14 by 476 and Justianian easly crushed what was left.

Questions: Answer those asked in connection with the
previous essay.
d. *History of civilization, early.* The question: "Nationalism has long been a force in European history.
There were already signs of it in the period A.D. 1200–
1550. What were some of these signs? Name your
grade for this answer.

1 If nationalism is defined as a spirit of cultural unity and the fact
2 of political unity among a people who speak the same language
3 and live in the same area, then some European people were
4 nationalistic (and others were not) in the Late Middle Ages.

5 Politics: the French monarchy began to centralize visibly under
6 Louis IX and Phillip Augustus (13th century) and even stub-
7 born areas like Burgundy were ruled from Paris by 1550; Spain
8 was under one monarch by 1500; the English were slower and
9 Civil War slowed them down but the Tudors (beginning in
10 1485) were nationalistic in plan and policy. Germany and Italy
11 were not unified politically because they kept the medieval
12 ideals of Empire and Papacy. Culture: Renaissance painters
13 and poets, such as Petrarch in Italy, Erasmus in Holland,
14 Shakespeare in England, Ronsard in France all used national-
15 istic themes. Economics: some countries tried to centralize their
16 economic and protect the nation, such as England. There was
17 plenty of nationalism in that period but not as much as later
        TIME

Questions: This fellow wrote a fairly decent answer,
seldom misspelling a word or erring in grammar. He
had a good topic sentence (where is it?), but the essay
is hardly perfect.

1. Which of the following faults does the essay contain? In what ways, however, is its construction
   superior to the preceding essays? (i) inadequate
   paragraph construction, (ii) poor sentence structure, (iii) general imbalance as an answer to the
   question

2. In which of the following ways is it inadequate as
   written history? State where each occurs: (i)
   error of fact, (ii) questionable interpretation,
   (iii) inadequate definition of terms, (iv) dis-
   orderly narration or chronology, (v) tenuous
   causal explanation, (vi) omission of key material

3. What are the pros and cons of writing "time" at
   the end of an essay? What might be some better
   alternatives?

e. *History of civilization, recent.* The question: "In what ways did the Enlightenment function as a backdrop to the French Revolution?" Name your grade for this answer.

1 The Enlightenment backdropped the Revolution in many
2 ways. Some of these ways are the following. Writers and intel-
3 lectuals (!) wrote so as to shake up the people who read them.
4 Such people included alexander, Pope, Voltair, and others.
5 They swept aside the intellectual rubbish that piled up for
6 centuries and then the Rev. came in 1776 people were ready
7 for a clean sweep. Other things were wars, especially that
8 France had with everyone, especially Britain and Germany.
9 Constitutionally limited monarchy and rule by the consent of
10 the governed, as advanced by Montesquieu and Rousseau, pro-
11 vided the moderate revolutionaries of '89 with extremely
12 important intellectual underpinnings. Then the whole thing
13 exploded, because of the Enlightment.

Questions: Answer those asked regarding essay [b]. Are there any signs of plagiarism in this one? What is plagiarism?

f. *United States history before 1865.* Question: "In the 1840s did government more generally support, regulate, harass, cooperate with, or ignore private enterprise?" Name your grade.

1 State governments did a lot of regulating in the 1840s. Often
2 they regulated canals and steamboats. Also they helped build
3 roads, most banks were state banks. Manufacturing they ig-
4 nored. Local governments did much the same, which one would

5 expect since they were created by the states and had no sover-
6 eignty of their own. The United States, or federal government
7 was much less powerful then than it is now; either in sheer size
8 or in comparison with the states. However, it's tariff policies,
9 it's land policies, it's monetary policies, its rivers and har-
10 bors projects, all meant cooperation and support of private
11 business. But it didn't do the regulating as it later would, in the
12 I.C.C. and antitrust laws. Its hard to generalize about support,
13 regulation and ect. except to say that they didn't ignore each
14 other certainly.

Question: Rewrite the passage, with an eye to cor-
recting any historical or compositional faults it may
have. Reorganize it if necessary, but do not, except
for needed corrections, add any new information or
ideas, and do not omit any information or ideas the
essay now contains, except what is extraneous to the
main argument. Work out a topic sentence, and be
sure your essay has a beginning, a body, and a conclusion.

3: DIGGING

THERE ARE MANY excellent books that can help you write
clear, effective, concise, and acceptable English. Two of them
that are widely available and that go beyond the dictionary
and the basic grammar book are William Strunk and E. B.
White, *The Elements of Style* (New York: Macmillan Company, 1959), and H. W. Fowler, *A Dictionary of Modern
English Usage* (various publishers and dates). Language facility and language study, like many other things, is fascinating
if you're good at it and very dull if you're not. These two books
are so well done, however, that they will probably ensnare you

into better usage even if writing is not one of your strong
points.

4: HOMEWORK

RESURRECT YOUR LAST history examination. Undefensively
and without regret, rewrite two or three of the least felicitous
paragraphs with an eye toward removing any of the compositional and historical faults discussed in this section.

TWELVE

HISTORICAL NARRATION

1: BACKGROUND

FORMAL LOGIC, AS it was first codified by the renowned Greek philosopher Aristotle (384–322 B.C.), involved a number of rules designed to insure the logical accuracy of statements. Aristotelian logic centered around a linguistic structure called the syllogism, in which the truth of a statement was insured by its deduction from other statements already known to be true. The classic syllogism began with a general statement called the "major premise," which was known to be true from observation, definition, or other syllogisms. It continued with a "minor premise," another known statement which used one of the terms of the major premise but which referred to a particular thing. Then the syllogism ended with a conclusion, which put together the remaining terms of the major and minor premises. The example often given in the old logic books was this: "All men are mortal" (major premise); "John is a man" (minor premise); therefore, "John is mortal" (conclusion). The syllogism worked well, and it still does when one wants to deduce something from something already known. Problems arise, however, when one must deal with things not known for certain. Formal logic had rules covering statements that properly began with "probably," "perhaps," or "it sometimes but not always happens that . . ."; but it dealt much more adequately with statements that were inexorably certain than with statements that were only probable or conjectural. Of course, many statements in history, though not the most baldly factual ones, are only probable or conjectural.

Does this remove history from the realm of logic? Not at all. But it does complicate matters. Historical statements are not often black-or-white, absolutely certain or absolutely false. They are almost always some shade of gray. It is better to say, regarding a historical statement or analysis, that it has one "degree of truth" or another, a percentile ranking on a scale of truth content or certainty. One statement is very probably true, or most of it is certainly true, and has a truth content or certainty ranking of around 85 percent; another is less certain, or less of it is certain, and ranks around the 55 percent level. If historical statements, moreover, are only certain to a degree, then the ways in which they relate to each other are also certain only to a degree. History presents us with few syllogisms, not only because particular statements are not entirely certain, but the relation between them, the manner in which one can be deduced from a preceding one, is not certain either. Nevertheless, there is a logic in historical writing.

The rules of this historical logic are by no means as straightforward as the rules of Aristotelian formal logic and probably will never be set down on paper. Even if they could be set down, they would probably be too complicated to apply accurately; and, even if they were applied, the historical writing that resulted might well be unreadable. You may have gained a contrary impression, but historians do attempt to write interestingly, and an excess of rules would almost surely prevent this. Logic in historical writing, however, is a quality that may be difficult to define but is not hard to identify. There is undeniably such a thing as a "flow of ideas" in anything that is written, and that includes history. In well-written history, one idea seems to flow logically from those that went before and leads easily into those that follow. What the writer has done in these happy cases is to put his ideas or statements about the past in an order that seems normal to his reader. The evidences of the past, having been absorbed and ordered by the historian's conscious mind, take shape on the written page in such a way that the conscious mind of the reader easily makes sense of them.

Certain kinds of historical statements have a built-in crutch which helps them ambulate logically with greater ease than almost any other kind of writing. This crutch is chronology. It is obvious to anyone that the statement, "Lenin, Trotsky, and the Bolsheviki in the late fall of 1917 overthrew the Kerensky régime, and in the spring of that year Kerensky and others then forced the Czar to become a constitutional monarch," is not logical. A prior action, as in that sentence, is made to depend on a later action, which is not possible. There may be few certain rules in history, but one of them is that later events cannot cause earlier events: time moves in only one direction. Later events often change the *significance* of earlier events in the minds of historians writing still later, but clearly the Bolshevik revolution in late 1917 could not in any way have been the cause of the liberal revolution in early 1917. The lesson here is that when a historian is dealing with events that are concrete and visible and that happened at a definite time and place, he has the benefit of chronology in helping to make his story logical.

But if the Russian revolutions of 1917 were events whose

facts were concrete, visible, and rather definite, such events as the industrialization of Russia, the spread of revolutionary ideas, the changing nature of social groups and classes in the Russian cities, are not so concrete, visible, and definite. We have already discussed the distinction between histories that deal with the short-term, clear-cut event and histories that deal with long-term, complex social or economic or intellectual events. Not only do these two kinds of history differ with regard to questions of truth or objectivity, but they also involve different writing problems. If we deal with economic change in Russia between the freeing of the serfs in 1861 and the revolutions of 1917, or the diffusion of the ideas of Marx, Plekhanov, Lenin, and others through the *intelligentsya* from 1890 to 1917, or even the impact of the World War on Russia from 1914 onward, we are in a position where chronology can help us much less. What will really count in dealing with these historical problems is a logic of ideas. One topic must flow from the preceding one and then flow logically into the next. There are as many techniques for achieving this as there are good writers; each has his own methods; each practices his craft as his experience and intelligence tell him it can best be practiced. Some writers begin with general observations and proceed to the particular; others begin with specific statements and built inductively to greater and greater heights, revealing the significance of their subject matter to the reader gradually; others have still other ways of handling this writing problem.

Some historical works appear to have little to do with narration, since they are organized not according to a chronological pattern but according to topics or problems. For example, suppose you have in hand two books about the American presidency in the nineteenth century. One opens with a chapter on Thomas Jefferson and continues with successive chapters on the administrations of Madison, Monroe,

J. Q. Adams, Jackson, and so forth. The second begins with a chapter on the nominating process and proceeds with successive chapters on electoral politics, party machines, the cabinet, the presidents' relations with the Senate, et cetera. Because the first is organized chronologically and the second topically does not mean that the second is not history, as long as the second bears such qualities of written history as fidelity to the sources, an organized pattern of events, and, above all, a consideration of *change over time*. Chronological organization is not an essential earmark of history. A topically organized work will, in fact, presuppose a chronological (and narrative) structure but present its historical material in a topical or problem-oriented form in order to achieve greater clarity, in the author's view.

In the final analysis each historical topic will have its own form of narration and will organize itself in the mind of the historian in the way he thinks most logical. If he is skillful, and perhaps also lucky, his logic will be the reader's logic. Then his history will have been well written.

2: FEEDBACK

THE FOLLOWING SENTENCES are garbled versions of historical paragraphs. There is a right way, sometimes a nearly-right way, and many wrong ways to string these sentences together into coherent historical statements. You should be able to put them in order—which is the same as saying that you should be able to see the logic in them. Two guidelines may help: remember that chronology may be there to help you, on the ground that a later thing cannot influence an earlier thing, and look for general statements or topic sentences, and then build the paragraphs around them. (You may find the key to the original order of the paragraphs at the end of section thirteen, below. Work out your reconstruction first, as best you can, and when you are finished compare it with the original. Note where and why the author's narrative logic differs from yours.)

    a. These sentences appeared in a textbook in American history used in high schools in the United States over a hundred years ago (S. G. Goodrich, *A Pictorial History of the United States* [Philadelphia: E. H. Butler and Company, 1865], pp. 198–199). They concern certain events in 1775. They are given here out of their original order, but the geography and chronology contained in them should help to indicate their proper order.

1. Four major-generals, to serve under Washington, were also appointed.
2. He received his commission four days afterward.
3. When Washington reached Cambridge, the British forces in Boston amounted to eleven thousand five hundred.
4. The appointment of Washington, as commander-in-chief of the army, was made on the 15th of June.
5. Washington, as soon as he had taken a survey of the whole ground, called a council of war.
6. In company with Generals Lee and Schuyler, he left Philadelphia for the north on the 21st of June, and, after a little delay in New York—where he left General Schuyler—he arrived at Cambridge, near Boston, on the 2d of July.

    Questions: (i) What is the proper order of the sentences? (ii) Where does the chronology help, and where geography, in deciding?

    b. Most of these sentences describe social change in late nineteenth-century America. In this case the proper order of the statements is not clearly indicated by geography or chronology but depends more upon grammatical logic and the subordination of specific to general ideas.

1. These three great areas of economic life depended for their growth, to be sure, not only on "great men" but on the labor of millions.

2. Several transcontinental railroads were built and other lines criss-crossed the country.

3. This was an age of industrialization and urbanization in some ways unmatched in American history.

4. Investment bankers developed new techniques of business organization and of capital formation.

5. The United States from 1865 to 1900 experienced a great growth in cities and in industry.

6. Andrew Jackson, meanwhile, was aghast.

7. Powerful individuals such as William H. Vanderbilt, Andrew Carnegie, and J. Pierpont Morgan captured the country's imagination while developing the three great sectors of capitalistic enterprise: transportation, manufacturing, and finance.

8. American manufactured products not only satisfied many domestic needs, but exports of them increased too.

9. The problem which the generation after 1900 therefore had to meet was that of preserving the industrial and urban development of the 1865–1900 years, while extending its benefits to the mass of the people.

10. English economic growth, once far ahead of that of the United States, began to level off in comparison.

11. Yet these millions very often received less in the way of direct benefits from an expanding economy than they did of low dollar returns for their labor, wretched living conditions, and physical insecurity.

Questions: (i) One statement does not belong with the others at all. Which is it? (ii) One statement is not necessary to a logical flow and could easily be left out. Which is it? (iii) List the numbers of the remaining nine statements as they should occur in proper sequence.

c. Besides the logic built on chronology and the logic of terms and ideas, there is another kind of logic which sometimes appears in historical writing. This is the logic implied in rhetorical language. Since the appeal of rhetoric is more aesthetic than intellectual, the rules of its logic are even fewer than usual. The following is a passage, in a garbled version, or rhetorical history, of a kind for which writers strove in the late nineteenth century. (From Ferdinand Gregorovius, *History of the City of Rome in the Middle Ages,* translated from the fourth German edition by Annie Hamilton [London: George Bell and Sons, 1894], vol. 1, pp. 125–126.)

1. Her very name was to her a power.
2. The Sibylline books, which had been found in Alexandria in the time of the Antonines, had announced the downfall of the city after the speedy appearance of Antichrist, who was expected to return from the ends of the earth in the form of the inhuman monster, the persecutor of the Christians, the matricide Nero.
3. The Apocalypse prophesied the fall of this great Babylon which had made all nations drunk with the wine of her pleasure.
4. It was only fanatical Christians who regarded her with horror as the seat of idolatry.
5. The Palladium of Rome would then have lost its power, if the might of the city and of the glorious Latin race had not arisen again through Christianity.
6. In opposition to Virgil, the Fathers of the Church, Tertullian and Cyprian, asserted that the Empire of the Romans, like the dominion of the Persians, Medes, Egyptians and Macedonians, which had preceded it, so far from being imperishable, was hastening to its end, and legend relates that even Constantine, summoned by an oracle, had built the new Rome by the Bos-

phorus because ancient Rome was doomed to destruction.

7. The ideas, "Rome" and "Roman," were impressed on the system of the universe.

8. Although, by means of long and bloody wars, she had brought so many nations into subjection, she had never inspired hatred; for all, even the barbarians, were proud to call themselves Roman citizens.

9. Even although she had ceased to be the seat of the Emperor and of the highest officials of state, she remained the ideal centre of the Empire.

10. The city was still the embodiment of civilization, the Palladium of mankind.

> Questions: None of the sentences are "fakes"; all of them appear in Gregorovius's original paragraph, though of course in different order. Arrange them in their original form. Are there alternative reconstructions? Which seems best?
>
> d. The following passage, from a recently published textbook, involves a logic of chronology and of ideas. It concerns the economic theories of John Maynard Keynes (1883–1946), as published by Keynes in 1936, which have profoundly influenced capitalist and developing countries ever since. (From J. Russell Major, *The Western World: Renaissance to the Present* [Philadelphia: J. B. Lippincott Company, 1966], p. 851.)

1. If business was sluggish, it should be stimulated by increasing the amount of money available to the producer and consumer.

2. Keynes pointed out that in liberal economic thought production and prices depended on the law of supply and demand as they were related to gold.

3. Thus, both the discovery of precious metals in the New World in the sixteenth century and the failure to discover important

new gold mines between the California strike of 1849 and the Klondike strike of 1896 had been the result of chance; yet both had affected the economy: the sixteenth-century discovery of precious metals by causing a rapid rise in prices, and the late nineteenth-century failure to make any significant discovery of gold by causing a slow decline in prices.

4. The quantity of gold, however, varied with the discovery and operation of gold mines, and not with the needs of the economy.

5. If business was optimistically investing at a rate that threatened to produce an inflationary boom to be followed by the inevitable bust, it should be checked by reducing the quantity of money available.

6. What Keynes proposed was that gold and currency be divorced and that the quantity of money in circulation vary with the needs of the economy rather than the supply of gold.

Questions: (i) Put the sentences in their best and proper order. (ii) Are there alternative reconstructions? (iii) What elements intrinsic in the sentences demand that they each follow a particular sentence and that each be succeeded by a particular one and not some other one? (iv) Chronology, the logic of ideas, and the necessities of language all play a part; where?

3: HOMEWORK

DEFINE, IN TWENTY words or less, the phrase "the logic of historical narration."

THIRTEEN

QUANTIFICATION AND UNIQUENESS IN HISTORY

1: BACKGROUND

THE THREE PREVIOUS sections have explored the very close relation that exists between history and language. The historian, we found, must have considerable verbal skill. We now need to take account of the fact that an ability to deal with quantities and a certain amount of statistical skill will help him greatly too. This is because many facts, although unique from one standpoint, are so similar that they can be grouped and counted (for example, the fact that you were born is critically important and unique in your own experience, but it is perfectly possible and probably useful to include it among millions of others in plotting population trends).

There has been a strong trend in recent years, particularly among historians of the United States but others as well, in the direction of applying quantitative techniques to the writing of history. More and more, as historians have dealt with long-term trends in the past or have attempted to unravel the nature of past institutions and problems as these traveled through time, they have found quantification—grouping similar facts and manipulating them mathematically—to be an extremely important tool. The pioneering work in the use of quantitative techniques was done in the social sciences, such as political science, sociology, and economics, and, of course, statistics, the discipline which developed the very tools of quantification, is generally regarded nowadays as being a kind of bridge between mathematics and the social sciences. Historians, however, never bashful about appropriating the findings and techniques of other fields, have successfully borrowed many of the devices of quantification from statistics and the social sciences as they once borrowed precepts from philosophers and theologians. The historians have bet that if sociologists, political scientists, and others in the social sciences found quantification so helpful for analyzing present-day human behavior, then quantitative techniques ought to be helpful for analyzing human behavior in the past. The bet has paid off, and historical writing has been enriched enormously by it.

Quantification has helped historians on a wide range of fronts. Economic history was probably the first to benefit from the trend. Economic historians have been using quantification for so long—at least three-quarters of a century under modern statistical conditions—that it is second nature to them and virtually indispensable to their craft. In the academic life of certain major European countries, in fact, economic history has been considered a field separate from "straight" history, largely because of the centrality of statistical techniques in the training and work of economic historians. Today the trend is more pronounced than ever among economic historians, and they not only analyze price trends, wage scales, national income, international trade patterns, national and worldwide cycles of prosperity and depression, and other problems as they have been doing for some time, but they also have kept abreast of the increasingly influential branch of economics called econometrics, which involves such fascinating problems as the construction of mathematical models of whole economies for given time periods.

If the economic historian cannot function without knowing and applying quantitative techniques, these techniques are also becoming hardly less important for social and political historians. Social historians have been able to apply statistical techniques to new kinds of evidence in order to describe the group structure of past societies, the movement of peoples across land and sea regions and from towns to cities (this sort of study is now a branch of history in itself, called "historical demography"), changes in social attitudes and values, such as nationalism, assimilation of outside groups (crucial to the study of American immigration, for example), and religious values over time-spans in the past, and many other problems. In all these cases, the gathering and analyzing, with the accuracy of statistical tools, of quantitative data has increased immensely the confidence with which we can now discuss the shape and development of many past societies. Much work remains to be done, but the application of quantitative techniques in social history is unquestionably a wave of the future.

Political history is in a similar situation. Who, in a congress or a parliament, voted for what? From what areas and groups did the "yea" and "nay" votes come? Do the "yea" and "nay" votes on certain measures correspond statistically to particular ethnic, racial, sectional, or economic characteristics of geographical areas? What were the trends of voting in public elections? What generalizations can we make about the kinds of people who have sought careers in public life, and how have the origins and training of public men changed over periods of years? From what parts of society have political parties and pressure groups gained their support, and how has this support changed over a time-span? These are questions that political historians often ask nowadays, and quantitative techniques have become of prime importance in finding the answers. (For some actual examples of quantitative research topics recently undertaken in the United States, see the "Digging" section of this chapter.)

There has even been a trend toward the use of quantification among intellectual historians, paralleling the trend among economic, social, and political historians. Historians of ideas and historians who make it their business to plot the attitudes of mind of people in the past naturally use, as sources, statements—usually written—left by those past people. How often did certain concepts or ideas or attitudes arise, relative to other concepts, in the expressions of those past people? What were they thinking about on certain questions? Intellectual historians, influenced in part by literary scholars who have also done this, have applied "content analysis"—counting and correlating the frequency with which certain words and concepts appear in given bodies of sources—to find out what those past people were thinking about.

2: COMPUTERS AND HISTORY

FOR ALL OF THESE historians who today find quantitative techniques useful, very considerable help has come from those mysterious brainchildren of modern technology, the computers. Intellectual historians engaged in "content analysis" find their work eased tremendously by electronic scanning devices, which can locate on a page a word or a phrase which has been pre-fed into the machine, without the researcher having to pore over piles of pages in search of a mention of his quarry. Scanning machines can be used similarly by political historians or biographers who must look through large bodies of sources (for example, a fifty-year run of a daily newspaper) for passing references to their subject. Without such a machine, historians must (and always have had to) undertake a kind of drudgery which is essential—since the source must be looked at—but which is really a waste of their skills. Scanning machines do not substitute for the human mind, but they do substitute for the human eye, thereby saving the owner of the eye a great deal of time in which he can use his mind, which no electronic device can duplicate or replace.

Computers serve the historian in a similar way—as drudgery-cutters. No matter how large or advanced or speedy a computer may be, it can really perform only two tasks. It can do basic arithmetic, saving the researcher enormous amounts of time that he must otherwise spend in adding, subtracting, multiplying, and dividing. Secondly, it can remember very large quantities of information, which is stored within a large computer on electronic tape, ready for accurate recall upon an electronic signal.

Suppose, for example, that a researcher in American history wants to know if voters in large cities have gradually, over a time period, come to support the presidential candidates of one political party significantly more than those of the other major party. He can feed into the computer the two-party voting returns for certain cities, selected specially or at random, and (for comparative purposes) the two-party voting returns for smaller cities or for rural areas, over a time-span (let us say, for twelve presidential elections). The computer can work out the percentage of support for each party in each area in each election with extreme rapidity; all the computer does it simple arithmetic, but the thousands of long-division problems involved in the project would take the researcher himself an inordinate amount of time.

Suppose further that the researcher wanted to know whether a certain immigrant group (German-Americans, for example) have shifted in their support of one party over the same time-span, and if there is any difference between the political behavior of German-Americans in cities and those in rural areas. If the computer has been programmed so that it has stored on tape the location of heavily German-American voting districts in certain states, and then the computer is fed with voting returns from these districts, it can recall the information about the voting districts and correlate it with the voting data, producing information which the researcher can describe in words, or in tables, or trace on a graph. Such results normally will have a considerably higher degree of confidence than the impressions a researcher would get from, say, the newspapers of those voting districts or the isolated remarks of a few commentators at the time.

The computer has not done the researcher's thinking for him, but it has saved him huge amounts of labor that he would have had to expend in arithmetical computations. The uses to which computers can be put by political, social, and economic historians are only beginning to be uncovered. The possibilities and programs for European, African, Asian, Latin-American, ancient, and other branches of history are just as great as they are for United States history. With the continued development of computer technology, historians will find the problems that they can analyze feasibly growing more and more numerous. Since the computer can deal only with what is fed into it, and since what is fed into it will depend on the historian, the computer in no way reduces the essential need for the conscious mind of the historian or the essential need for sources. Historians using computers, in fact, are still unable in most cases to achieve the kind of certainty that social researchers like to have, because the historian's quantitative data—his sources—tend to thin out the farther back he goes in time, and there are gaps even in rather recent collections of quantitative data, just as there are in other kinds of sources. Nevertheless, the computer-equipped historian is in a position to use quantitative evidence and to analyze it in ways that his predecessors could not do, simply because they were understandably overwhelmed by the mass of arithmetical labor required to make sense of that evidence.

Does the use of quantitative techniques render obsolete the history that deals with unique events or with individual people? Does it "dehumanize" history by dealing with masses and quantities rather than with units? Some people still think so, but they are letting their fears run away with them. In the first place, no computer or computer-equipped historian will, as a result of computer technology, improve upon the classic narrative histories of Thucydides, Gibbon, or Parkman; no mathematical technique will render obsolete the biographical powers of such modern masters as a Christopher Hibbert (Mussolini, Garibaldi) or a Douglas Southall Freeman (George Washington, Robert E. Lee). There is plenty of room, and always will be, for histories that deal with events of the concrete, visible sort. For these people, quantitative techniques are not so useful. Even the historians who deal with long-term trends are not all helped by quantification, and even those who are must still depend on their conscious minds and their literary skills if they wish to make their findings presentable. The computer, the scanning device, and statistical methods themselves are tools, and nothing more; they write no history, they do no thinking by themselves. They are a marvelous help to some; a useless piece of machinery to others. To those who can use such tools, however, they open up a new world of research possibilities.

3: FEEDBACK

WHICH OF THE following research problems might benefit

from the use of quantitative techniques, in whole or in part? How?

1. Whether the rate of desertions was higher in the Russian or the Austrian armies in World War I. (Example: Find the size of the armies, the number of desertions in each, compute percentages, and compare.)

2. Whether ammunition or food supplies had any bearing on desertion rates. (This is much more complex and would demand nonquantitative as well as quantitative data, plus carefully controlled correlations of the latter.)

3. Whether Machiavelli looked at statecraft as completely amoral.

4. Whether economic growth has been as rapid in Russia as in Britain.

5. Whether a developing country such as Nigeria has been undergoing anything like the growth the United States experienced at an early period in its national history.

6. Whether the increasing proportion of city dwellers in America has had any effects on political preferences.

7. Whether intellectual leadership in America has been drawn from the same kind of social background as in the past, or has been changing.

8. Whether American historians are using quantitative techniques more than they once did.

4: DIGGING

SEVERAL VERY HELPFUL guides to historical quantification now exist. Here are some:

Benson, Lee. *Toward the Scientific Study of History: Selected Essays*. Philadelphia: J. B. Lippincott Company, 1972.

A collection of pieces, going back to the mid-fifties, by a historian who has been a leading advocate and practitioner of quantification.

Dollar, Charles M., and Richard J. Jensen. *Historian's Guide to Statistics: Quantitative Analysis and Historical Research.* New York: Holt, Rinehart, and Winston, 1971. A unique handbook on the tools of quantification and how to use them. Contains a first-rate bibliography, including both American and non-American items.

Historical Methods Newsletter. A quarterly publication put out by the Department of History, University of Pittsburgh; began in December, 1967. Contains articles (e.g., "The Historical Study of Vertical Mobility," "Availability of Manuscript Census Records," "Statistics Textbooks for Upper-Level Classes in Quantitative History," "The Occupations of the Ante-Bellum Rich," etc.), book reviews, news of interest to quantifiers, and descriptions of research projects (e.g., "The Liberated Woman of 1914," "a multivariate analysis of the career patterns, social activities, and political attitudes of 7,000 prominent . . . women"; "The Structure and Growth of Port Cities: A Comparative Study of Liverpool and Boston"; "The Nature of Black Poverty in Southeastern Pennsylvania, 1780–1860"; "Psychological Thought within the Context of the Scientific Revolution, 1665–1700"; "Crime and Punishment in Puritan Massachusetts Bay," etc.).

Rowney, Don Karl, and James Q. Graham, Jr. *Quantitative History: Selected Readings in the Quantitative Analysis of Historical Data.* Homewood, Ill.: Dorsey Press, 1969. An anthology of articles on quantification.

5: HOMEWORK

a. Name a number of types of historical sources that are

particularly suited to analysis by quantitative techniques.

b. Locate the United States Census in your college library, and locate a statistical publication by a foreign government or by the United Nations. Where do you find it? What is the call number? How are these documents organized and divided?

KEY TO THE "GARBLED PARAGRAPHS" IN SECTION TWELVE

a. Paragraph from Goodrich's *Pictorial History:* Proper order is 4, 2, 1, 6, 3, 5.

b. Paragraph on social change in late nineteenth-century America: Sentence completely out: 6. Sentence which might be omitted entirely, but could appear between 3 and 7: 10. Proper order of the remaining sentences: 5, 3, 7, 2, 8, 4, 1, 11, 9.

c. Paragraph from Gregorovius: Proper order is 10, 9, 1, 7, 8, 4, 3, 2, 5, 6.

d. Paragraph from Major: Proper order is 2, 4, 3, 6, 5, 1.

FOURTEEN

HISTORIANS, SCIENTISTS, AND ARTISTS

1: BACKGROUND

"Is HISTORY AN art or a science?" Few questions have been asked more often, and few questions used to agitate historians as much as this one. In the nineteenth century, when the historical profession was in its adolescence in the Western world, the profession sought painfully, as an adolescent might, for security and certainty. Looking around in haste, the profession saw that such certainty did seem to belong to science, and, thereupon, history, too, began to call itself scientific. Elaborate explanations and forthright assertions of the scientific quality of history appeared in Europe and America. History was not alone in this, for the belief in the boundlessness of exact science was very widely prevalent in the Western world at that time. And in truth, the historians of that day were able, in many respects, to demonstrate that their way of studying the past was more certain, definite, and systematic than that of their predecessors. History had been looked upon for ages as a branch of philosophy, ethics, and literature. But to the scientifically inclined nineteenth-century mind, this was not enough. History should be scientific, and historians struggled to make it so. But they were never really able to convince the mass of generally educated people, the so-called "intelligent laymen," that history was a science and that literature and history no longer had any connection. Most people went on believing and buying and reading the historians who could produce written history that had more literary grace than a laboratory report. Which side was right? Was history an art, or was it a science?

The answer seems today to be "neither and both." In the last few decades, the historians themselves have severely limited their former claims to scientific certainty, while the mass of "intelligent laymen" want something more definite from the history they read than flights of poetic fancy or a more adult version of the moralizing of Aesop's *Fables*. Ask historians today whether history is art or science, and most will reply, probably, that it is scientific in its method and artistic in its execution; in other words, do your research scientifically, but write it artistically. There is much truth to this, but it is not the whole story.

Let us compare the methods and subject matter of a historian, a physicist, and a novelist with respect to a few common problems. All three begin at the same place—with a question. For each, something needs explaining. But the thing to be explained is very different. For the physicist, it may be the behavior of liquids and gases; for the historian of concrete events, a war. For another historian, it may be something more abstract than a war, perhaps a long-term event such as a price trend or a social phenomenon such as the treatment of children over a time-span. For the novelist, the thing to be explained will be a private vision about some kind of human action. The differences among these very different subjects lead to differences among the physicist's, historian's, and novelist's ways of approaching their tasks. Where do they get their evidence? Respectively, from the results of laboratory experiments, from a hodgepodge of written and oral records, from personal observation. How do they observe what they are studying? The physicist observes it through instrumentation under controlled conditions in a laboratory; while he cannot observe a subatomic particle directly, he can see its photographic evidences, and most important for the purposes of our distinction, he can recreate at will the situation in which such evidences appear. The novelist makes direct observation of people in daily life and from his memory; if he wishes to know more about how people behave in certain kinds of situations, he can go out and observe such situations. The historian, however, observes the sources that just happen to remain extant. His contact with his subject is at second hand, and unlike a physicist he cannot recreate a situation in which more sources are created.

The fact that the sources intervene between the historian and his subject matter raises questions for him that the others do not have to face. He must verify his sources and combine and judge them intelligently in order to become as certain as he can that they are accurately representing the past to him. Depending on what kind of sources he finds and what parts of them he selects, he will be helped by "scientific rules of evidence," which are really the collective experience of past historians about how to evaluate and deal with different kinds of source materials. This may be "science," but many historians would be content to call it "craft." Here is one place where the historian faces a problem that neither the physicist nor the novelist faces; he cannot confront his subject matter directly, but must do so through the mediation of his sources.

But what about the question of how definite or compelling is the evidence for each man? In this the historian resembles the physicist more than the novelist. The novelist's impressions, observations, and experience are relatively unfixed. His subject matter is, or can be, constantly in flux. But the physicist's evidence is stable: if water freezes at 0° Centigrade, and a certain liquid does not freeze at 0° Centigrade, then it cannot be water. Frequently, though not always, the historian enjoys such stability too. If he can show from his evidence that a certain group of people in England averaged £500 annual income in 1850 while the national average might have been £100, and that this group now averages £1500 while the national average may be £1000, he can safely and definitely conclude that this group is relatively less well off than it was over a century ago. Historical evidence can very often, though not always, show with almost total certainty that some things are true and others are not true.

In two other ways, however, the historian is closer to the novelist than to the physicist. In the first place, he cannot change the conditions under which his subject matter behaves, whereas the physicist can. A historian of the Russian Revolution cannot repeat the Russian Revolution without the factor of World War I being present, in order to see whether World War I had any effect on the revolution; he has got to accept the revolution as it happened, and it happened only once. The chemist can, on the other hand, observe the behavior of certain gases and liquids in many ways, under different temperatures, in combination with different outside substances, and with different electrical charges; his observations have repeatability. The physicist can also find the boiling point of a new substance, for example, very definitely and accurately by boiling it a repeated number of times. The historian cannot locate the "boiling point" of revolutions in general by bringing France in 1789 or Russia in 1917 to boil a repeated number of times. He must deal with unique occurrences.

The second way in which the historian approaches the novelist more than the physicist is in mode of presentation.

The physicist is much less dependent upon written language and will express his findings to a large extent in mathematical terms, but the novelist and the historian cannot express themselves at all without language. Einstein revolutionized physics in a few short articles, but it took many hundreds of moving pages for Parkman to write the history of France and England in North America or for Tolstoy to write his classic novel of the Napoleonic Wars.

These are some of the major ways (there are others) in which history compares with physics and fiction. For practical purposes, we can say that history is neither a science nor an art, but something different from either one. It is a discipline, a body of knowledge, and a human activity unique and independent. Unlike physics or creative literature, it has a subject matter and a way of dealing with that subject matter that is not purely scientific or purely artistic. Like the sciences and the arts, however, history depends on the conscious minds of its practitioners in order to make communicable sense of the part of the universe with which it deals.

2: FEEDBACK

   a. History and science. Reflect for a moment on your own experiences in high school or in college or otherwise with the study of science—chemistry, zoology, geology, or whatever.

   1. Are the data—the "facts"—used in these fields like the data used in the writing of history? Are they more concrete? More easily verifiable? Are scientific facts more "objective" in that they are perhaps less prone to twisting by the observer's experience or bias? (You will probably find that different kinds of scientific evidence and different kinds of historical evidence will produce varying answers to these questions.)

2. What do scientists mean by a "control situation"? Does it help them to verify their conclusions?

3. Are there "control situations" in history? Is it really possible, for example, to say whether post–Civil War Reconstruction in America would have been different if Lincoln had lived or whether the world would have been any different if the United Nations had not been in existence since 1945?

4. Does it make any difference, with regard to the certainty of their conclusions, that scientists are generally in direct contact with the things they study, and the historian must examine his subject matter only at second hand, through the medium of the sources?

5. Is it true to say, then, that the study and writing of history are generally a more creative process than scientific study, but that they bring less certain results? How do history and science compare with regard to the complexity of their subject matter and the degree of personal judgment that the historian and the scientist must necessarily exercise?

b. *History and literature*. Literature takes many forms, and among them are lyric poems, epics, plays, essays, and novels. Some examples of these may appear to be partly historical; for example, Homer's epic poem the *Iliad,* Shakespeare's play *Richard III,* or historical novels such as Walter Edmond's *Drums along the Mohawk,* Ole Rolvaag's *Giants in the Earth,* and Joseph Heller's *Catch-22*. But there are differences between literature and history.

1. In writing a novel, historical or otherwise, where does the novelist get his material?

2. Does a novelist need to use sources, documents, or data in the same way that a historian does?

3. We have seen that historians must be creative, in the sense that written history involves some interpretation and judgment. We assume that literature involves creative activity. Aside from involvement with documents, is there anything else that might differentiate a historian from a historical novelist or from a poet?

3: DIGGING

MANY PEOPLE HAVE written about the relation or lack of it that history may bear to science and art. These are recent discussions that are succinct.

Morison, Samuel Eliot. *History as a Literary Art: An Appeal to Young Historians*. Old South Leaflets, series II, no. 1. Boston: Old South Association, n.d.

Walsh, W. H. *Philosophy of History: An Introduction*. New York: Harper and Brothers, 1960. See Chapter 2, "History and the Sciences."

Lipset, Seymour Martin, and Richard Hofstadter, eds. *Sociology and History: Methods*. New York: Basic Books, 1968. See especially the opening two chapters by the editors.

4: HOMEWORK

a. Briefly list three ways in which the historian resembles and three ways in which he differs from (i) an experimental scientist and (ii) an artist, literary or otherwise.

FIFTEEN

HISTORY AND HOPE

1: BACKGROUND

YOU NOW KNOW something about the nature and uses of history and the problems that historians face when they attempt to find out what happened in the past and to convey what is significant about it. You now realize that the past is not self-evident, that it has to be sought after carefully and unceasingly, and that this job is not simple or easy. But you should know too that it ought to be done, for otherwise people would have learned nothing from their mistakes and triumphs and would face blindly the fog and darkness of the future without light to guide them.

True, the torch of history is a flickering torch, and the future it must light is vast. The historian knows this, but he knows that some light is better than no light, and he knows that his job is to make that light as bright as it can possibly be. He knows that what he finds in the past will be only as significant as the questions he asks of the past. He knows that even the best questions must sometimes remain unanswered because the past has left no sources with which to build an answer. He knows that his judgment may not be up to the task of judging which sources can answer his questions best and how he ought to derive significant order from them. He knows, finally, that because of the nature of historical research itself, he can never achieve the degree of certainty and absolute truth that he— and his readers or listeners—would like to have. When his history is finished, he must reassure the timorous that it is indeed possible to learn something about human behavior that may help us to understand where we are and where we are going; he must also disappoint the impatient who want to know these things immediately and with absolute certainty.

As any historian knows, history has its uses, and it also has its limits. The study of history warns us to be cautious, to make haste slowly, to forego our natural demands for certain knowledge and confident prediction. History reminds us that people are complex and not very predictable and that to judge them or even to hope to understand them involves a measure of prudence and insight that does not come naturally. History can teach these habits of mind, nonetheless, and they are as necessary for understanding the present as they are for making sense out of the past.

This is, of course, because the past is simply a collection of presents that have already happened. The past is just as complicated, just as broad, and just as confusing as the present. The historian takes pride in having as his special province an area of just such immensity, and he is mindful of the fact that it is his discipline that has the job of synthesizing a myriad of events, individuals, cultures, trends—whatever people have done. History may be messy, it may be uncertain, and it may be difficult; but it is still the one great synthesizing discipline. That in itself is enough compensation for the uncertainties and the difficulties.

A great historian will be, therefore, a man of many virtues.

He will be a careful craftsman, skilled in the location, verification, and evaluation of sources. Wisdom and understanding about people, since past people are his subjects, will be his. Comprehension of his own time he will have to have, since without such comprehension he could never ask significant questions of the past. He will be patient and prudent, because he knows that some secrets of the past can never be unveiled. But he will be full of hope, realizing that man, who has undergone many ordeals and setbacks and achieved a few triumphs, has still survived. The historian can help man to survive a little more easily, a little more confidently and hopefully. The life of the past is the light of the present.

2: DISCUSSION

WHAT HAS THE study of history so far taught you about people or about yourself?

How much of the present is new?

How much of America is like or unlike the rest of the world?

How much are you like your grandparents?

APPENDIX I

A FEW HELPFUL BOOKS

THIS IS A very brief list of helpful works on historical method, on historical writing, and on philosophical questions that arise in historical study. Many other good ones also exist. Some of the following have bibliographies which cover their subjects extensively.

1: BOOKS ON HISTORICAL METHODS AND THE WRITING OF HISTORY

Barzun, Jacques, and Henry A. Graff. *The Modern Researcher*. New York: Harcourt, Brace, and Company, 1957.

Benson, Lee. *Toward the Scientific Study of History: Selected Essays*. Philadelphia: J. B. Lippincott Company, 1972.

Berkhofer, Robert F., Jr. *A Behavioral Approach to Historical Analysis*. New York: Free Press, 1969.

Dollar, Charles M., and Richard J. Jensen. *Historian's Guide to Statistics: Quantitative Analysis and Historical Research*.

New York: Holt, Rinehart, and Winston, 1971.

Gottschalk, Louis. *Understanding History.* New York: Alfred A. Knopf, 1950.

Gray, Wood, and others. *Historian's Handbook.* Second edition. Boston: Houghton Mifflin Company, 1964.

Gustavson, Carl G. *A Preface to History.* New York: McGraw-Hill Book Company, 1955.

Hexter, J. H. *Doing History.* Bloomington: Indiana University Press, 1971.

Higham, John. *Writing American History: Essays on Modern Scholarship.* Bloomington: Indiana University Press, 1970.

Kent, Sherman. *Writing History.* New York: Appleton-Century-Crofts, 1941.

Nevins, Allan. *The Gateway to History.* New York: D. Appleton-Century Company, 1938.

2: GENERAL REFERENCE WORKS THAT NO HISTORIAN SHOULD BE WITHOUT

A good dictionary; preferably an unabridged, but at least a reliable smaller one such as Webster's *Collegiate* or the *American College Dictionary.*

Bartlett, John. *Familiar Quotations.* Thirteenth edition. Boston: Little, Brown, and Company, 1955 (or other editions).

Fowler, H. W. *A Dictionary of Modern English Usage.* Oxford: At the Clarendon Press, 1959 (and other years).

Strunk, William, and E. B. White. *The Elements of Style.* New York: Macmillan Company, 1959.

Turabian, Kate A. *A Manual for Writers of Term Papers, Theses, and Dissertations.* Chicago: University of Chicago Press, 1955.

3: BOOKS ABOUT THE PROFESSION OF HISTORY

American Historical Association. *History as a Career, to Undergraduates Choosing a Profession.* Washington: American Historical Association, 1961. Pamphlet available from the American Historical Association, 400 A St., S.E., Washington, D.C. 20003.

Daedalus, issue of Winter, 1971, entitled "Historical Studies Today," and issue of Spring, 1971, entitled "The Historian and the World of the Twentieth Century."

Shafer, Boyd C., and others. *Historical Study in the West: France, Great Britain, Western Germany, the United States.* New York: Appleton-Century-Crofts, 1968.

Perkins, Dexter, and John L. Snell. *The Education of Historians in the United States.* New York: McGraw-Hill Book Company, 1962.

4: BOOKS ON THE PHILOSOPHY OF HISTORY

Danto, Arthur C. *Analytical Philosophy of History.* Cambridge: At the University Press, 1965.

Gardiner, Patrick. *Theories of History.* Glencoe, Ill.: Free Press, 1959.

Meyerhoff, Hans, ed. *The Philosophy of History in Our Time.* Garden City, N.Y.: Doubleday and Company, 1959.

Stern, Fritz. *Varieties of History, from Voltaire to the Present.* New York: Meridian Books, 1956.

Walsh, W. H. *Philosophy of History: An Introduction.* New York: Harper and Brothers, 1960.

NOTES, OUTLINES, AND THE FAIL-SAFE STUDY SESSION

1: THE NEED FOR NOTES

THIS SECTION AND the following one are concerned with helping you to succeed if you really try. To be a successful history student you need to practice a certain kind of economics; you are confronted with certain resources—lectures, discussions, textbooks, the library—and your job is to make these resources go as far as you possibly can with the time and intelligence at your disposal. Because the available historical materials that deal with the history of civilization or even the history of the United States are practically endless, certainly far more extensive than you can hope to cope with in a semester or two, you need to find some answer to that ancient question in historical study: *What is important?*

What follows are some guidelines which should help you make more of your visible resources as a college history student. They may seem very elementary, and indeed they are, but their simplicity derives from the distillation of experience. The first dictum of experience is the necessity of organization.

In matters intellectual, it happens that you *can* add to your stature one cubit by taking thought. A few minutes' thought given over to organizing the material from lectures, texts, discussions, and library materials can save you from a great deal of drudgery.

Class lectures are the means by which your professor conveys to you what he thinks are the most important and most interesting aspects of the subject matter of the history course in which you and he are participating. Because of the breadth and variety of history, no two lecturers will stress exactly the same points throughout a course. Because judgments may reasonably differ, there may be divergences of opinion even between the lecturer and the textbook in the same course. In any event, you should know what is happening in the course lectures and have some organized record of what has happened. You should, in short, take notes.

Like other study habits, note-taking is perfected only after long experience. This is all the more reason why it should be undertaken early. The first thing to remember, with regard to note-taking, is to come to class and to come on time. But then what? The next step is to listen intelligently. Shorthand experts and speed writers sometimes appear in history courses and transcribe everything a lecturer says, but although such athletic enterprises are impressive, there still comes the moment of truth when even verbatim transcriptions of lectures must be boiled down to their principal and most memorable points. At some American institutions a student can buy a "canned" set of lecture notes, but this kind of short-circuiting of education can bring a student to grief if he happens to have one of the many professors who wouldn't be caught dead teaching a course exactly the same way twice. The only safe procedure is to attend class and listen carefully, noting the general subject of the lecture, the principal divisions or topics it includes, the lecturer's main judgments, and the main pieces of evidence (or at least the unfamiliar pieces) the lecturer cites in support of these judgments.

Although as a general rule it is better to take too many notes than too few, wholesale transcription isn't normally the best method. There are anecdotes about students, usually girls, who seat themselves with pencil poised over paper waiting for the lecture to begin; lecturer arrives, says "good morning"; student writes "good morning," top left of first page. If the student waits at least until the lecturer announces what he is going to talk about and how he plans to proceed, the note-book will be a little less cluttered and a little more useful.

As is the case in many areas of historical study, the technique is to reflect on what is going on. Ask yourself questions. What is important here? What is it that the lecturer is trying to convey? (He may not always convey it very well, but that does not mean you should ignore it.) What are the principal points of the lecture, and—very significant to ask—how does each main thought connect with the preceding one and the following one? What is the sequence of ideas? In any lecture, there will be a great many details, points of fact, or figures of speech; the more of these you remember, the better. But pay primary attention to the *principal* topics and the *logic* of the ideas.

After a class ends, the note-taking process is really only half done. To get the maximum value from your lectures, you should not only take intelligent notes but make intelligent use of them. A few hours after the end of the class, after you have gone to other classes or attended to other things but while the history lecture is still somewhat fresh in your mind, read over your notes for legibility and continuity. They may not be quite as clear as you thought when you took them; insert a few phrases or additions so that the connections of the main points are clearer, and make sure that these main points stand out distinctly. Another shrewd move is to compare your notes with someone else's, preferably someone more accustomed to note-taking or more knowledgeable about the course. If you are a freshman, acquaint yourself with an upperclassman in the course and borrow his notes, or if you are doing only A— work, borrow the notes of someone who is earning a clean A. If there is some point you've missed or don't understand, by all means avail yourself of the professor's office hours for a visit and clarification. (Find out when the hours are, and if the professor is chronically not there, complain.)

Examinations are ªa periodic experience which you probably regard with horror or at best as a necessary evil. They may be such, but you should also think of them as an educational opportunity. They force you to do something healthy— to reorganize and relearn a significant segment of your course. The lecture material will probably play a significant part in any examination, and you, therefore, should work over your course notes in preparation for the examination. The first thing to do is to construct a short, half-page or one-page summation of the main points of all the lectures. This is simply another way of organizing the course material into a thoughtful pattern, and a thoughtful pattern is what you need most, not only for the examination but in order to learn the material well. Do your notes make any sense? Is there any system to them? Do they provide, really, a brief synopsis of the important points of the lectures? They should if you've taken them intelligently, then gone over them later in the day of the class, then compated them with the notes of other students, and sought clarifications of elusive points. Another extremely helpful practice in preparing for examinations is to compare notes, visually and verbally, with two or three other members of the class.

2: OUTLINING: THEORY AND PRACTICE

ONE OFTEN HEARS history professors say, seriously, that you don't need to remember everything you read, but only the important things. But they don't tell you how to tell the important things from the others.

The reason for their reticence is that it is really difficult to state what the important things are going to be. The important things cannot be predicted, as a rule, from general principles. Sometimes it is possible to read a paragraph and pick out a "topic sentence," but not every writer has a topic sentence in every paragraph. There is, frankly, no single overriding rule by which one can discover a priori what is "important" in a paragraph or sentence or book, but you are still expected to learn the "important" things.

There is a way out of this dilemma—the use of brief outlines for chapters or major segments of chapters or class notes. These outlines force you to find out what, in general, the author was talking about. Sometimes authors aren't sure, and in such cases outlining or any other form of analysis does very little good. But it is to be hoped that the books you are using are not flawed in this way. You are attempting, in short, to ascertain and reduplicate the *structure* the author had in mind when he wrote his book. Such a restructuring must be brief if it is to be of any use; a chapter should be outlined into no more than three to six major divisions, with each of these including very few subdivisions. If you outline more extensively, you obscure with too much detail the main elements or outlines of the chapter.

When you discover how to determine the author's general structure, you will have developed a technique for reading any book more intelligently. Neither a textbook nor any other book can be criticized until the reader has in front of him, either on paper or in the front of his mind, a brief and clear answer to the question: What is the overall subject of this book, and what major topics did the author think necessary to include in order to deal with that subject? Everyone knows how easy it is to read a book and remember nothing from it, but that is exposure, not education. Brief outlines will force you to put your mind to a book, and only this application of mind to the matter at hand, in this case a book, constitutes education. No one can educate you, not lectures or texts or other books; you have to do the hard work yourself of thinking through, of comprehending, these raw materials once they have been thrown in your path.

But if brief outlines can help in finding out what is "important" in books of all sorts, what about history books in particular?

Here we need to carry the general principle one or two steps further. Frequently you will find in historical writing that specific people or specific events are essential to the structure of the book or chapter with which you are concerned. This is not always true; much written history deals with groups of people and long-term trends rather than specific persons and events. But the unique fact is often essential, especially in books dealing with historical questions in biographical or narrative ways. In these instances, your outline—if it really captures the basic structure of the work—will organize itself around the key people and dates. The story won't be comprehensible without these key people and dates; you will have to take note of what is "important" because you'll have nothing but a jumble if you do anything else.

There may be occasions when you are required to learn nearly every name or date in a chapter or a book. But this is not as painful as one may think, and, of course, since history deals so often with specific data, the more data you know, the better, regardless of whether or not you are expected to go beyond the raw data to the structure of historical problems. In these cases, you simply have to memorize.

Nevertheless, what you do with the data—how you organize and structure the facts—is at least as essential as the data themselves. This is true for you, and it is true for the author of the most factual, seemingly cut-and-dried lecture or text-book. In reading, as in writing and lecturing, history must be understood and carried on as a process of the human mind, a process whereby the mind selects and then makes sense of the evidences of the past.

Now put this theory into practice.

a. Prepare a one-page outline of the class notes you have accumulated so far. Be sure it is an *outline,* stating the general topic first, then its main divisions, and within each main division the major subdivisions. Here is a model:

Title (e.g., European Expansion into the New World)

    I. Main topic (one of three or four, perhaps; e.g., European background)

    A. Principal subtopic (e.g., Renaissance expansiveness)

        1. Subdivision (accumulation of investment capital)

        2. Subdivision (desire for new trade routes)

           a. further subdivision (overland routes)

           b. further subdivision (water routes)

              i. further subdivision (South and East: Da Gama and others)

              ii. further subdivision (westward: Columbus)

        3. Subdivision (nationalism)

               a. further subdivision (unification of Aragon, Castile, and Granada)

       B. Principal subtopic (sixteenth-century religious upheavals)

           1. . . . n. Subdivisions

    II. Main topic (availability of the Western Hemisphere)

       A. Principal subtopic (Pre-Columbian civilizations)

           1. . . . n. Subdivisions

       B. Principal subtopic (European voyages before 1492)

           1. Subdivision (St. Brendan, A.D. 800?)

           2. Subdivision (Norsemen, ca. A.D. 1000)

       C. Principal subtopic (nautical and geographic technology)

    III. . . . n. More main topics, subtopics, etc. (By the way, what do "e.g.," "i.e.," and "ca." mean? Look them up in an unabridged dictionary.)

The main function of an outline is not to include everything in the course or even all of the data you would do well to remember, but to organize and classify the important points so that you will recall them more easily and, above all, relate them logically.

b. Prepare a one-page outline of the last chapter assigned for your next examination—the fourth chapter, for example, if chapters one through four have been assigned.

c. Compare your several chapter outlines, which you should have completed by now, with the outlines you have made of your class notes. Do they resemble each other at any points? If they do not, the reason is probably that your instructor sees connections between parts of the material that you still do not see. He will probably expect you to make these connections. Prepare another outline, but a short one, which combines and organizes your lecture and text materials together, and which shows some sensible relation between the two.

The main thing you should be finding is the structure of the course material. It is this, not a long list of unconnected facts, that is "what is important."

3: THE TEXTBOOK

THE PURPOSE OF your textbook and such accompanying books as you may have is to present you, compactly and in black and white, with the essential information and interpretations of the material of your course. Textbooks are essentially course-oriented reference guides. No matter how much lecture material or outside reading you may be expected to do, the fact that your course involves a textbook and possibly other books, perhaps paperbacks, indicates that there is some basic information with which your instructor will assume you are familiar. You will have to "know the book." The following are a few tips that should help you do this economically.

1. Read over your textbook quickly in large portions when they are first assigned. Read several chapters or the whole book at one time, without attempting to remember everything, but trying to discover and keep in mind the major themes and the major segments.

2. Go back and read the first chapter slowly. After you read each paragraph of that chapter, ask yourself what it was about. Actually set the book down and pose that question. Then, jot down on paper, in your own words, your answer; then, look over the paragraph and find the sentence that comes closest to your answer. Bracket it or underline it; it is the topic

sentence. If there is no topic sentence, but you are still convinced that your answer is correct, jot down your answer in the margin. (Don't worry about the resale value of the book. Marking it up in this way will lose you perhaps two dollars at the end of the term if you sell the book on the secondhand market. Consider the two dollars as the price of admission. In any case it is a lot less than the rewards you will get from high achievement.)

3. After you have read the first chapter and have done your jotting and bracketing: (i) Read through the chapter, skipping everything except the key sentences. (ii) Then ask yourself what the author was writing about in this chapter. What was it that was important? (iii) Write an essay of only thirty to forty words answering those questions. (iv) Put in outline form, on about one-half of one side of a piece of paper, a summary of the chapter. Note well, when you write this outline, as with any other: never write down a sentence or topic heading unless it is in your own words. Copying chapter headings or marginal phrases from the book does almost no good at all. Follow the same procedure for each succeeding chapter.

4. Now for the payoff. Four days before an examination, read over the chapters to be covered, paying special attention to the key sentences.

5. And, two days before an examination, read your brief essays and outlines of each of the chapters. Study them thoroughly, as well as any paragraphs either of extreme importance or about which you are unsure. After you have done this, you ought to be confident of the material and well prepared for the examination.

All of this takes time and effort, and with practice you may find that you can, with equally good results, cut some corners. But compare the time these procedures take with the time you must spend in language or mathematics exercises or the time that you must spend in laboratories for science courses, and you will agree that it is simply a matter of giving your history course its due.

4: SUPPLEMENTARY READINGS AND PROBLEMS

MORE EXTENDED HINTS about how to succeed when writing book reports will follow in Appendix III, but a few comments on supplementary readings should help you in the early stages of your course.

When you are confronted with a required or recommended book or a historical problem on which you must report, use much the same technique as that discussed with regard to textbooks, except in shorter form. Note the key sentences, or write some of your own if the author has been too discursive. Do not, of course, put marks in a book if it belongs to someone else or to a library. The main thing here is not to attempt to memorize the book you have read, but to ask of yourself and of the book, after each chapter and again after finishing the book: (i) What was the author trying to talk about? What was he attempting to communicate? (ii) Who is the author, and where did he get his information—did he base his opinions on solid sources, and was he independent of bias? How far, in other words, can he be trusted?, (iii) How well did he succeed in accomplishing what he was apparently trying to do? Was the book convincing at all points, and if not, where and why not? (iv) Of what value, if any, was this book in helping you to understand the subject matter of the course? How does it relate to the matter of the course, and does it raise important questions about the text or the lectures?

Again, obviously, the important thing you should be doing —some popular opinion to the contrary notwithstanding—is thinking through a considerable body of material, not just trying to memorize it cold. Your outside readings ought to bear significantly on the subject matter of the course, and they ought to be integrated with it in your own mind. Otherwise you've chosen the wrong readings and failed to handle them properly.

5: PREPARING FOR EXAMINATIONS

AN EXAMINATION IS no more than a device to find out how well you understand and can cope with the main themes of the course. How can you prepare for an examination most effectively and economically?

The stealing of examinations is a practice highly frowned upon in academic circles. Fortunately it is rather rare. It is always grounds for expulsion from a college or university with very little chance of being readmitted there or elsewhere, and it is often a criminal offense. The practice is not recommended. A time-honored technique, however, which is indeed highly recommended, and which time has not withered nor custom staled, nor which is *verboten,* is that of using one's ingenuity to predict what questions will be included on an examination. (One of the uses of history, in fact, is the scrutinizing of a professor's past examinations in the hope of being better able to prophesy what his future ones will be like.) Accurate prediction of this sort is a skill and therefore takes some practice. Here are some guidelines for intelligent outguessing:

1. From the textbook and lecture material assigned for your next examination, list—and do no more than list—the most important people from among all those mentioned and covered. The sheer process of deciding which are the critical ones will teach you something of the material. Do you know two or three facts about each of these persons—enough to identify them positively and unmistakably?

2. Do the same for the most important events from among all the "facts" and "dates" for which you are responsible.

Why, in your judgment, are they important—i.e., what is their significance in the totality of the subject matter—or why are they at least more important than the other facts and dates?

3. After you have studied your text and lecture notes and what notes you may have taken on outside readings, get together with two or three other people taking the course (at any rate, not more than four others) on the evening before the examination. This is your fail-safe procedure.

By that time you should have your own ideas of the material well in mind. But you may be overlooking some important points, or you may have missed some obvious but key connection. Before you go into your study session, formulate three questions (each of them ten or fifteen words long), each of which would demand a comprehensive knowledge of the whole subject matter to be covered and which would need to be answered in an essay of one hundred to three hundred words. Then make a brief outline of a good answer. This will force you to synthesize the most important trends and problems; the tougher your questions, the more they will help you. Also formulate several questions to cover single aspects of the subject matter, questions that would be answerable in a short essay of fifty to 125 words. Make a brief outline, verbal or written, of these questions. If your colleagues do the same, you will have a good agenda for your discussions. Discuss these questions. Revise them or evolve new ones which your group agrees are likely to appear on the examination. Think of how these questions might best be answered, and discuss the answers as well. Pay at least as much attention to organizing and synthesizing as to the memorizing of factual data. How the facts are related means at least as much as the facts themselves.

You may not predict the test questions precisely, but you will surely be able to answer more confidently and intelligently any question that does appear.

WRITTEN HISTORY: SOME HINTS ABOUT EXAMINATIONS, REPORTS, AND PAPERS

1: BACKGROUND

WHAT FOLLOWS IS some very practical advice, aimed at helping you proceed more successfully through the history course you are taking. It should also help you make more economical use of your time, in the sense of getting greater achievement out of the hours you spend on your course.

You are probably convinced by now that the writing of history is a very complex affair, to be undertaken only by mature scholars, and in a sense you are right. But a good product demands a good beginning. Your instructor is going to insist that you write history in the form of examinations, in the form, perhaps, of book reports, and possibly also in the form of a term paper or theme. Considering the difficulties involved in historical writing, these can look like formidable tasks. Can you possibly do an adequate job of it? Of course not, if by "adequate job" you mean a finished product of mature scholarship. You can do an adequate job, however, in view of the time, sources, skill, and energy that an instructor may reasonably expect of you. Here are a few simple rules that will greatly improve any form of written history and a few that apply especially to examinations and book reports.

1. Think before you write. Pose these questions to yourself, and answer them in your own mind before you start writing: What is my subject? Where should I start, and where should I stop? What are the two, three, or four major organizing ideas—the principal points that I ought to be making and around which the data and lesser points should be built?

2. Organize your material logically. A very brief outline is your greatest aid in doing this, and you should jot down a very brief outline before you write an examination answer or a book report.

3. Make sure you have an introduction, a body, and a conclusion to your essay, regardless of its size. In the introduction, tell what you are going to do; in the body, do it, proceeding from your first major point and all of its supporting ideas and data to your second major point, and so on; in the conclusion, tell what you have done, by summarizing your major points and showing how they satisfy the question or problem with which you set out to deal. In a one-paragraph essay question on an examination, the introduction and conclusion may be no longer than a sentence or even a clause; in a two- or three-page report, they may each run a full paragraph by themselves. But all three parts should appear, and the introduction and conclusion together should be no more than half as long as the body of the answer or report.

4. Avoid errors in grammar and spelling. Be sure that each sentence and each paragraph has an acceptable structure, and be sure that it relates clearly to the whole exercise. (A study of Section Eleven should help teach you how to do this and show you what mistakes especially to avoid.)

Now for some special cases of written history.

Examinations require the application of these four rules,

but under peculiar circumstances. Usually you will be pressed for time; you will ordinarily not be able to consult books, notes, or sources and will have to rely on the adequacy of your studying. So:

1. A day or two before you take an examination, follow the recommendations in Appendix II with regard to examinations.

2. After you sit down to take the examination, being well rested, well informed, and well provided with paper, pen, and ink, read over all of the questions. Read the instructions carefully. This glance over the examination, before you begin to write, will give you some idea of how you should allot your time. If you have a choice of questions, decide which of them you will answer and how much time and space you should give to each. Be sure you answer any question that is required, and be sure you answer no more and no fewer of the questions than the examination calls for. Many students begin history courses with the mistaken idea that if they answer more questions than they have to, they will get extra credit; or if they answer fewer questions than are demanded but at greater length, this will do as well as answering the number called for. These are grave blunders. Usually the instructor has designed the examination so that a good student can answer just as many questions, no more and no fewer, than are asked for in the amount of time available in which to answer them. Two essays taking fifteen minutes will not ordinarily satisfy an instructor who has asked for one thirty-minute essay; he will simply disregard one of the fifteen-minute essays and consider the other one half-done and probably half-baked.

3. Before you try to answer any question, read it over *very* carefully, several times. Many hideous *gaffes* on examinations stem not from lack of knowledge or even lack of organizing ability but from answering some other question than the question that was asked or ignoring some important part of the

question. Many questions that appear on essay examinations have more than one part; be sure you answer all of them. Your instructor is looking for certain definite things and has very probably expended considerable time and effort composing an examination that will let him know whether you know what is going on in the course. He will not be amused if you answer what you feel like rather than what he wants or if you omit parts of questions.

4. In connection with this, don't write "TIME" at the end of a half-finished examination or uncompleted last question. The instructor will not believe you, because (rightly or wrongly) he will feel that the examination he designed to be completed in an hour *can* be finished in an hour by a competent person, and he will get the idea that you are too lazy and sloppy to finish the job you started. If you really are cramped for time at the end of an examination and the papers begin to be collected before you can finish, write a concluding last sentence which will serve as a summary (see above, general hint number 3) to the question you are working on.

5. Before you answer any question, jot down on scratch paper or in a margin a very brief outline of your answer and perhaps a very few major facts or organizing concepts that you think you might forget. The watchword here, of course, is organization. Two minutes spent in organizing an essay will probably save five to ten minutes of sloppy or irrelevant writing and will lessen the chance that your essay may end up on some ideological pinnacle other than the one you wanted to climb. These errors, moreover, are ones that your instructor will consider unimpressive, to say the least.

6. Always support your generalizations with specific facts. Indeed, your generalizations, like any historian's, ought to flow easily and with seeming inevitability out of the facts you present. A few pious platitudes or glittering generalities will not get you very far in history.

7. Also, don't depend on any bias or predilection you think you see in your instructor to get you a good grade if only you can slant your answer in the same direction. Be honest. To be otherwise is an insult to yourself and to the instructor. There have been cases of left-leaning instructors who might downgrade a right-leaning essay and right-wing instructors who might flunk liberals. But happily they are very few. Students who complain of such discrimination very frequently lack in addition the moral courage to ask themselves whether a low grade wasn't the result of poor organization, sloppy English, or insufficient knowledge.

8. When you write an essay or a report, don't get careless, and don't get fancy. Write clearly, carefully, and concisely. This will help 'convince your instructor that you have an orderly and straightforward mind, and it will add a literary sheen to your writing that will impress a reader far more than a scattershot barrage of ideas, no matter how brilliant they seem to you, and far more than involuted and ornamented prose that you may think elegant.

9. Save a couple of minutes at the end of the examination period to glance over your paper for any obvious omissions of important points and for the correction of any grammatical errors or spelling blunders.

10. After the examination is over, relax, forget it, and hope for the best.

Book reports have a few rules of their own. A great many book reports are poor, largely for two reasons: the author of the report did not think, either about the book he read or about his report, and he did not organize his thoughts and therefore his report. Since every book is different and every book thus requires a different set of questions that must be asked of it, the rules for book-report writing must necessarily be general. But these will apply in one way or another:

1. Don't read a book "from cover to cover." Try it this

way instead, for this is the way experienced scholars have learned is very often the best way to read scholarly books. Read the title page first; then the table of contents, to see how the book is organized; then the bibliography, to see what sources the author used; then the preface, where he attempts to state what he is doing; then finally the body of the book. This scheme of reading will immediately provide tentative answers to five key questions, which you must be able to answer if you intend to have read the book intelligently:

(a) What was the author trying to do?

(b) How in general has he organized the book? What is its essential structure? What design of proof has he chosen in order to answer the question or problem to which he addresses himself?

(c) What did he use for sources—in other words, to what extent should you believe him?

(d) Who is the author? (It makes a difference, for example, in evaluating a book about Communism or the development of the Soviet Union, whether it was written by Trotsky, Stalin, Mao Tse-tung, J. Edgar Hoover, a traveler with no special background, or a historian or political scientist from the United States.)

(e) How well did the author succeed in doing what he set out to do?

2. Question (e) and perhaps some of the others will not be answered for you by the book itself. You will have to think about them. You will also have to decide for yourself the answer to a final and important question: In what way, if any, does this book relate to, add to, contradict, or support the subject matter of the history course for which you are reading it? There ought to be a helpful relation between the book and the course. For example, a book on Rommel and the Afrika Korps in North Africa in World War II or on the career of Napoleon may be a very fine book, but not for American his-

tory. On the other hand, a book on American military policy in World War II or on American-Soviet relations would be quite appropriate. The same is true for courses in the history of civilization. A good general rule for such courses is, unless you are instructed otherwise, to avoid books about American history.

3. Your written book report should contain the answers to these six questions. Here is a suggested order for a book report of five hundred words (which is the preferred length of book reviews in many historical journals and for many courses):

(a) At the top of the first page, a standard bibliographical entry for a book. This includes author, title, and facts of publication.

Example: Woodward, C. Vann. *The Burden of Southern History.* Baton Rouge: Louisiana State University Press, 1960.

Nearly all books will need no further identification, but if your book happens to be part of a series, one of several volumes, or of a certain edition, this should be indicated between the title and the place of publication.

Example: Smith, Adam. *An Inquiry into the Nature and Causes of the Wealth of Nations.* Edited, with notes, by J. R. M'Culloch. Edinburgh: Adam and Charles Black, 1863.

(b) One or two sentences—no more—answering succinctly the question, "What was the author trying to do?" This should occupy about twenty-five words.

(c) One or two sentences identifying the author, with attention to his other publications, his qualifications for writing this book, and his position or occupation (scholar, newspaperman, participant in the event he writes about, propagandist, representative of a special viewpoint, or whatever). This helps indicate his possible slant as well as his qualifications. This too should take about twenty-five words. Often the preface of the book will give you this information. Other places to look for identifications of authors are *Who's Who, Who's Who in America,* the French and other national editions of *Who's Who* for foreign authors, the *Directory of American Scholars* (in the fourth and current edition, Volume I deals with historians), *Contemporary Authors,* American and foreign biographical dictionaries, and other reference works.

(d) An answer to the question, "What sources did he use, and how well did he use them?" Did the author really use the materials he mentions in his bibliography or footnotes, or are they simply window dressing? Did the author ignore important sources? Does he omit source references altogether (and if so, why should you believe what he says)? This section should take about fifty words.

(e) A *brief* summary of the book, telling how it is organized. No more than a hundred words here.

(f) An evaluation of the book in about 250 words. This is the main part of your review, the section in which you think originally about the book you read. Here you answer in depth the question, "Did the author accomplish what he set out to do?" What did he do especially well? What did he do poorly? Does he disagree in significant respects with what you know of the subject already, from textbook, lectures, or other reading? If so, do you agree with him or with what you learned elsewhere, and why? Does his writing style help or hinder the reader's understanding and absorbing of the book's content? From the literary and historical standpoints, does he prove his case? How original is it?

(g) A brief conclusion, in about fifty words, stating whether, how, and to whom the book is useful and, in particular, whether or how it is helpful to a student in your course.

4. After you have written the report, rewrite it as may be necessary to improve the style and organization. Finally, make sure that it is clear of any errors of spelling, grammar, and acceptable usage.

Term papers vary even more than book reports. A term paper is essentially a small-scale research project, and the rules that apply to it are essentially the rules that, when followed, expedite a project in historical research such as a master's or Ph.D. dissertation or a book. The term paper will be shorter, less complex, and less thorough with regard to the sources than the more advanced projects, but the steps involved are much the same. Your term paper, no matter how brief, will benefit from the observance of the rules that many historians follow in executing more refined and advanced research problems. These are the chief steps in the research process, and they apply to problems of very different magnitude, from term papers to large books.

1. Select your topic very carefully. You will have to decide at the outset whether your paper will be an attempt at original research, using primary sources for the most part, or a survey of the existing secondary literature on a relatively broad problem. In most undergraduate courses you will learn more from the latter approach, and this is probably what your instructor wants you to do. (Find out before you start.) In either case, however, your paper will benefit if its topic is defined more narrowly than broadly, and more specifically than generally. In a Western civilization course you may be intrigued by the impact of Greece upon Rome or by a comparison of the American, French, and Russian revolutions. You will find plenty to write about, however, if you take only one aspect of these problems; for example, "What in Roman sculpture was original, and what was borrowed from the Greeks?" or, "Did the presence of autocratic governments in Russia and France and the absence of it in America affect the

nature of the revolutions in those countries?" Even these topics are very broad, as you would quickly discover if you sought out what has been written on them. Limit your topic, and make it as precise as you can. Furthermore, state it in the form of a question. This helps greatly to keep your organization and your research relevant and to the point, and it gives you something to refer back to when you become uneasy about possibly drifting away from your original topic. The clearer and more precise your topic is in your own mind, the more time you will save and the more vivid and logical your paper will become.

2. As soon as you have a question in mind, the question being the topic of your paper—the problem you are going to try to answer—write it down and draw up a short but comprehensive outline of it. The outline serves as your "design of proof," the way you are choosing to answer the question, and at the same time serves to convince the reader that your answer is correct. This is a very major step. It is just as important as the very discovery of the topic, and it will be at least as difficult to perform. Many good paper topics and many good research projects fail because the researcher, although he is able to formulate a problem in a significant way, cannot follow through to the next step of designing an adequate way to answer the question he set himself. An outline will help you to do this, once you have asked a question properly, because it will allow you to see whether the parts of the paper you think appropriate at first glance really have any bearing on the problem and really do help you answer the question you have posed.

3. The third key step, after posing a problem and designing a way to attack it, is to survey the available sources. Do not start taking notes five minutes after you set foot in the library; if you do, most of the notes will later have to be redone or discarded. Find out, first, what sources exist within

your reach which will bear on the problem. Note what they are, what they look like, and where they are. For large-scale problems, you will want to use several depositories. You may find public documents in a university library; manuscripts in an archive, historical society, or large library; scholarly and reference works in these places or, sometimes, in specialized research libraries; unpublished local records in a county recorder's office; or some papers, perhaps, in the hands of a family or private individual. Your instructor will know the source depositories in your locality and can guide you to the most likely ones. Once you discover what sources are available and get a general idea of what they contain, you are ready to proceed to the fourth crucial step.

4. This step we can call "feedback." You are inevitably going to find, in virtually any historical project, either that the sources you want are not entirely available to support some of your ideas or some of the segments of your organizational scheme or, possibly, not even the basic problem itself. Or you will find that the sources demand a consideration of certain points that had not occurred to you at the outset. This is going to mean a change in your design of proof and perhaps even a substantial rephrasing of the question you initially set out to answer. What has happened is that you have set out to answer a certain preestablished question in certain ways. The sources don't quite fit that question and that pattern, but they will fit a revised question and pattern of proof. You have got to reach a kind of compromise with the sources by which you stick as closely as possible to what you originally set out to do but at the same time utilize the available sources and amend those parts of your question and design for which sources are not at hand. In doing this, you must be very careful not to give up too easily; certain questions or segments of your original design may in fact have sources that pertain to them, although at first glance these sources might have

escaped you. This underscores the need to make the third step, the search and survey of sources, very carefully. But after you have indeed made a thorough search and you do find sources you didn't think existed (or don't find other sources that you did hope were there), proceed to the next step.

5. This is simple: Redo your outline, and for each major segment of it indicate the sources that are pertinent. In other words, incorporate the feedback.

6. At this point you can begin to dig into your sources. Examine them thoroughly. Watch, too, for new sources that you missed on your original survey. And use your conscious mind to watch for further feedback; every time you examine a source and every time you take a note, ask yourself, "How does this information or idea help to answer my problem or any part of it, and how does this relate to or change the meaning of my other sources?" A moment's thought may save you half an hour of useless note-taking. Also, if some new bit of information seems to shed different light on what you've already done, don't be afraid to go back to your previously taken notes and do some reorganizing. You may have to recur to some sources you have already looked at; experienced historians have to do this frequently. If some new insight, idea, or relationship of one source to another occurs to you while you are taking your notes, write it down immediately. Such comments or asides will serve later to help you remember what your notes mean and how they should be put together, and they often serve as raw material for essential connective passages in your written draft.

A note on note-taking: There are, in general, two mechanical ways of taking notes. The first is to put them into bound copybooks, spiral notebooks, or otherwise on full sheets of paper, bound perhaps in a looseleaf notebook. Some people prefer this, and it is often thought to be the best way to take class notes. But for research it has the disadvantage of seducing you into putting several notes on a page, thereby rigidifying them in the order in which you took them. The second method is much more widely used among scholars; take your notes on file cards, which ordinarily come in three-by-five-, four-by-six-, and five-by-eight-inch sizes. If you put one note on a card, you can reshuffle that card with your other cards in the probable event that your organization will change to some extent by the time you want to write; the notes are just as readable as they would be in a notebook, and they are much more flexible. The note cards can be kept in a shoe box or other receptacle for quick reference. (You should also take separate notes for bibliography; see below under number 9.)

7. After you have taken your notes and exhausted your sources and meanwhile have digested what they mean and how they relate to each other and to your general plan and organization, you may want to devise a final outline which will, in fact, be the outline of the paper as you are going to write it. Perhaps you will be able to get by with an amended version of your original outline, but probably you will want to draw up a new one; the outline of a research project is not always the best outline for a paper, which should be literarily attractive as well as historically well researched.

8. Now write your paper. Again, be sure you have an introduction, body, and conclusion; be sure you proceed in the body from one major point to the next, in logical sequence. Some guidelines in the actual writing of historical papers: Do not quote extensively from your sources, and do not even paraphrase directly except in rare instances, and when you must, be absolutely sure you cite in a footnote the source you are quoting or paraphrasing; otherwise you may be guilty of plagiarism. As you begin each major segment of your paper, carefully study the notes that pertain to it and mull them over before you write. If you have absorbed them properly in your own mind and thought about what they should mean in re-

lation to each other and to the project, you will avoid much tedious flipping through your notes as you write; your writing will become much more fluent and readable as a result, and you will do the job much more quickly.

9. Footnoting and bibliography are essential parts of your paper. Don't worry greatly about them until you have a first draft completed, since writing out footnotes in full as you arrive at them in the writing process can interrupt fatally your flow of thought. A good device is to make up a separate set of notes as you research through your sources. This set of notes should contain the full bibliographical data on the sources you are studying. Thus, on the research notes themselves you need only state the author's name and also, if you are using more than one work by the same author, a couple of words from the title. Then as you write you can avoid stopping to make a full footnote entry and instead can make the same brief reference to the author and perhaps a title and, of course, the page number you are citing from the work. Put the note in brackets at the point where it occurs in your draft, and, then, if (as may well happen) you find you need to re-number your notes, none will get lost. When you are finished writing, you will go back and complete the footnoting and bibliography in proper style. They are important. Both the footnotes and the bibliography tell the reader, in effect, "If you don't care to take my word for this, here is where I got the information and where you may check it if you like." The bibliography serves this function for the paper in general, and the footnotes perform it for particular statements of little-known or questionable fact, of disputed interpretation, or of indebtedness to some other author for an idea. Footnotes and bibliography therefore serve very necessary purposes, although these functions are often obscured by the fuss made about the form they should take. Their standardized form is simply insurance that they will indeed perform their essential

function: to show the reader how to find, if he wants to find it, the exact work or page to which you are referring. There are dozens of types of standard bibliographical and footnote entries, but the following ones will cover the great majority you will make:

(a) For a book, bibliographical entry: author, then title, then series or volume number if appropriate, then facts of publication. Example: Daniel-Rops, H. *L'Eglise des Révolutions*. Histoire de l'Eglise du Christ, vol. 6. Paris: Librairie Arthème Fayard, 1960.

(b) For a book, footnote entry: essentially the same thing, except that the author's first name comes first, the facts of publication are in parentheses, and a page number is given since the reference is to a specific part of the book. Example: H. Daniel-Rops, *L'Eglise des Révolutions,* Histoire de l'Eglise du Christ, vol. 6 (Paris: Librairie Arthème Fayard, 1960), pp. 859–860.

(c) For a periodical reference, bibliographical entry: the article title is in quotes, and the journal in which it appeared is underscored; all of the pages included in the article are given. Example: Lampard, Eric E. "American Historians and the Study of Urbanization." *American Historical Review* 67 (October, 1961): 49–61.

(d) For a periodical reference, footnote entry: author's first name first; comma, not period, after the title of the article; only the page or pages specifically referred to are mentioned. Example: Eric E. Lampard, "American Historians and the Study of Urbanization," *American Historical Review* 67 (October, 1961): 59.

(e) For a government document, bibliographical entry: these can be confusing, but in general they follow the entry for a book. More attention needs to be given to the volume number and series name, since government documents very often appear as parts of a series. Example: U.S. Department of the Interior. Census Office. *Report on Population of the United States at the Eleventh Census, 1890.* Part I (Population), vol. 1. Washington: Government Printing Office, 1895.

(f) For a government document, footnote entry: differences in punctuation are similar to those for a book. Example: U.S. Department of the Interior, Census Office, *Report on Population of the United States at the Eleventh Census, 1890,* part I (Population), vol. 1 (Washington: Government Printing Office, 1895), pp. xxi–xxvi.

(g) For a second footnote citation of the same book: two gimmicks here. First, if the second citation comes immediately after the first, you simply write "Ibid." if it is the same page referred to, or "Ibid., p. x," if you are now referring to a different page in the same work. (*Ibid.* means *ibidem,* in Latin "the same.") Second, if some other citation intervenes between the first and the second citations of the same book, you need cite only the author's last name; also a brief version of the title if there is a chance of confusing this work with something else by the same author; then the abbreviation "op. cit." (Latin, *opus citatus,* the work cited); then the page referred to. Example: Daniel-Rops, op. cit., p. 843; or, U.S. Census Office, *Eleventh Census,* op. cit., pp. xlv-lii.

All this may seem very cumbersome, but standard forms like these show the reader that you have in fact used solid sources, and you are telling him where he may check up on you. Some of your references may be more complicated than these. If so, you should refer to a widely used handbook on these matters, such as Kate L. Turabian, *Manual for Writers of Reports, Term Papers, and Dissertations* (Chicago: University of Chicago Press, 1955), which is available in paperback.

Now for the final steps in your paper:

10. After you've completed your first draft, go over it very

carefully for correct English usage, for logic of organization, and (with reference to your subject) for inclusiveness. Condense or expand where appropriate. This is your second draft; you will probably need still a third.

11. The finished draft of your paper should include the following parts: (a) a title page indicating title, author, the course for which it is being offered, and the date of submission; (b) a table of contents; (c) the text of the paper, with footnotes either at the bottom of the pages or at the end of the text, depending on your instructor's goodwill; and (d) the bibliography. If you have other material, such as graphs, charts, tables, maps, or methodological appendices, refer to Turabian's *Manual* for instructions on their form and where they should be placed in the paper.

12. Be absolutely certain that your final draft is neatly typed and free from errors in English. It should be as simple, clear, terse, and fluent as you can make it, and it should have a logical structure which is visible to the reader. To accomplish this you may have to rewrite it in several drafts before you reach the final one, but it will be worth it. History is worth doing well.

2: HOMEWORK

THE FOLLOWING IS some drill work that you can do on your own, and which should help you gain practice in formulating answers to historical problems intelligently.

    a. Examinations. Suppose you were asked some of the following questions on an examination and were required to answer them in the time indicated. Give a brief outline of your answer to each question. In addition, write the first (introductory) and last (concluding and summarizing) paragraph to several of them.

1. Do you agree with the thesis that the Constitution represents a "conservative" reaction to the "liberalism" of the Declaration of Independence? (25 minutes)

2. Contrast the Jeffersonian and Jacksonian positions on internal improvements and on the tariff. (10 minutes)

3. Could the Civil War have been avoided? (one hour)

4. In what major ways were the problems facing President Wilson in 1914–17 and F. D. Roosevelt in 1939–41 similar, and in what ways were these problems different? (30 minutes)

5. Do you agree with the thesis, advanced by Edward Gibbon and others, that Christianity was primarily responsible for the fall of the Roman Empire in the West? Explain. (25 minutes)

6. What major evidences are there of anti-Western feeling in the Chinese Empire in the nineteenth century? (15 minutes)

7. Which cultural forces would you say have been of greater long-run significance in the history of West Africa: Arabic or French? (25 minutes)

8. Has the history of the world in the last century tended more to support or to contradict Marx's doctrine of proletarian revolution? (one hour)

b. *Book reports.* According to the admonitions given in earlier parts of this appendix as to what a good book report should include, outline (do not write fully) a book report on (i) your textbook and (ii) this book. In addition, write the first two and the last two sentences that these reports would include if you were to write them in full.

c. *Term papers.* Choose two of the following possible term paper topics:

1. The cultural impact of steam power in nineteenth-century America.
2. Is the term *Reconstruction* really a misnomer?
3. Recent views on the causes of the War of 1812.
4. Why America doesn't get along with China: a historical view.
5. Twentieth-century technology in newly independent African countries.
6. Napoleon and de Gaulle: a contrast of careers.
7. The novel as an instrument of social reform in modern Britain.
8. Non-Hebrew references to the events described in the Old Testament.

Then do the following:

1. Draw up a preliminary outline, a brief one, of the paper.
2. For each of the main parts of the outline, list the principal kinds of sources that you would expect to be useful (by a "kind of source" we mean government documents, manuscripts, newspapers, periodical articles, books—rather than specific items), and find in your library or in bibliographies one concretely useful example of each type of source.
3. Now that you have surveyed the available sources, draw up a revised outline of your paper, amending it according to the ways in which sources either are not available or are more abundant than you had suspected, and according to how sources seem to demand consideration of points you had not originally thought of. (This is that all-important "feedback" function.)
4. Transform your revised outline into a tentative table of contents, showing approximately how

much space you expect to devote to each segment. This will help to make your writing more concise and also to fix the paper more closely within its practical and required limits.

5. Choose one segment of your outline which you expect will develop into about two pages of finished manuscript. Research it and write it.

6. Rewrite, copy edit, and condense your pages as they may require.

7. Submit it and hope for the best.

INDEX